The First Kandyan War

The First Kandyan War

A Narrative & History of the British Conquest
of Ceylon

Narrative of the Operations of a Detachment
in an Expedition to Candy, in the Island of
Ceylon, in the Year 1804

Arthur Johnston

Extract from History of Ceylon

William Knighton

LEONAUR

The First Kandyan War
A Narrative & History of the British Conquest of Ceylon
Narrative of the Operations of a Detachment in an Expedition to Candy, in the Island
of Ceylon, in the Year 1804
by Arthur Johnston
Extract from History of Ceylon
by William Knighton

FIRST EDITION

First published under the titles
Narrative of the Operations of a Detachment in an Expedition to Candy, in the Island
of Ceylon, in the Year 1804
and
History of Ceylon

Leonaur is an imprint
of Oakpast Ltd

ISBN: 978-1-78282-289-9 (hardcover)
ISBN: 978-1-78282-290-5 (softcover)

http://www.leonaur.com

Publisher's Notes

The views expressed in this book are not necessarily
those of the publisher.

Contents

Narrative of the Operations of a Detachment in an Expedition to Candy, in the Island of Ceylon, in the Year 1804

Contents

To

His Excellency

Sir David Dundas, K.B.,

General and Commander-in-Chief, &c.

Sir,

The operations of any part of the British troops, and the means by which they may be rendered more effectual, cannot be a matter of indifference to the commander-in-chief. Whatever contributes to the improvement of military knowledge will, I am persuaded, be favourably received by your Excellency, to whom the service is already so much indebted for its present proficiency in military tactics. It is the object of this narrative to relate and explain a species of warfare in which the British troops have been little engaged, and are, consequently, less experienced than in European tactics. If I succeed in benefiting the public service, by showing in what manner the difficulties which pressed so severely on the detachment I had the honour to command may, in any future operations, be either removed or lessened, I shall feel myself amply repaid for the trouble I have taken; and shall, I trust, stand exculpated from the apparent presumption of having obtruded myself on your Excellency's attention.

I have the honour to be,

Sir,

Your most obedient humble servant,

A. Johnston,
Major, Third Ceylon Regiment.

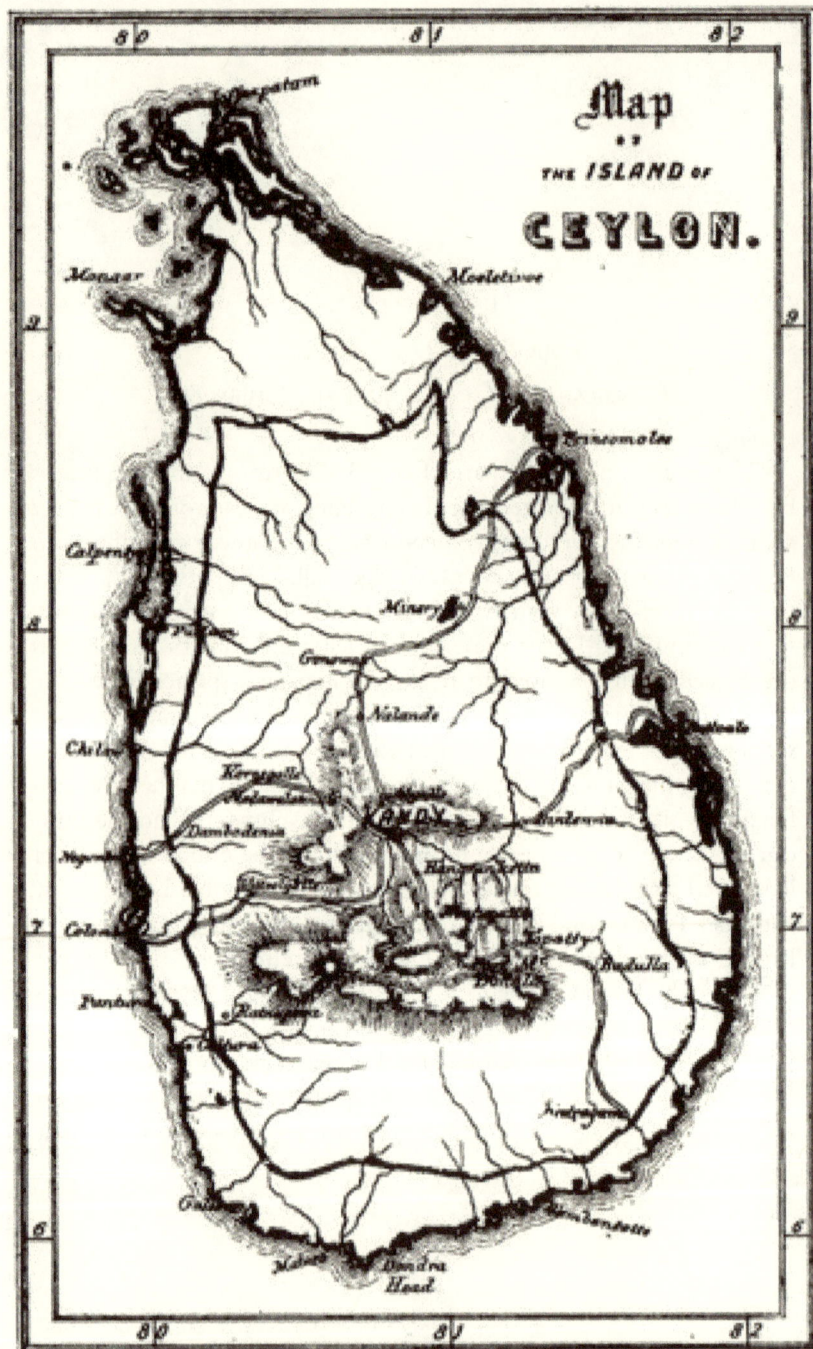

Map
OF
THE ISLAND OF
CEYLON.

EXPLANATION .... Boundary of the Maritime Provinces of Ceylon.

Preface

As it appears generally incumbent on those who offer information to the public, to explain the sources from whence they have derived their knowledge, it may not be improper to state the circumstances under which my experience on Ceylon was acquired.

In 1800 I commanded a corps of pioneers, which opened a road for General Macdowal's embassy to Candy. After that period, till the commencement of the Candian war, I was chiefly entrusted with the command of remote districts, uniting in my own person the civil and military authorities. On the breaking out of that war, in 1803, I was appointed to command a *free corps*, composed principally of Malays, and was generally employed in escorting supplies to and from the different *depôts*; a service which led to frequent skirmishes with the enemy.

When the army returned to Columbo and Trincomalé, after having seated Boodoo Sawmy (the prince whose cause the English espoused) on the throne of Candy, I was appointed first commissioner for regulating the affairs of the provinces ceded by that prince to the British Government. Illness, however, obliging me to repair to the sea-coast for the benefit of a change of air, I thus fortunately escaped the massacre which shortly after took place in the capital.

On the re-establishment of my health, I was appointed to command the district of Batticolo, which, in common with most of our other provinces, was invaded by the enemy, who was not driven out till after repeated skirmishes.

I continued at Batticolo till September 1804, when I received the instructions, in my conception of which originated the expedition to Candy, and which General Wemyss has obligingly permitted me to publish.

On my return to Columbo, I was nominated to the command of

Hambingtotte, into which the enemy had penetrated, under the Desave (chief) of Ouva, and from whence I was so fortunate as to expel them, with little loss on our side.

Thus, during a residence of nearly twelve years in Ceylon, the greater part of that time employed either in active military scenes, or in the discharge of civil duties, I had frequent opportunities of observing the nature of the country, and making myself acquainted with the character and customs of its inhabitants, and their mode of warfare.

Having been led, since my return to Europe, to consider the importance of the Island of Ceylon as a colony, which, I trust, will never again revert to the enemies of Britain, I have been induced to commit to the press what occurred to my observation during my continuance there, in the hope of promoting the benefit of His Majesty's service; by giving to officers, who may hereafter be employed in the interior of the island, that information which they may not have had the means of obtaining, in regard to a species of warfare peculiar to it, and which has not, to my knowledge, been noticed in any former work.

In publishing this narrative I aspire to no literary fame, having joined the army at the age of fifteen—too young to have made any considerable proficiency in letters—and at an age when men are even apt to lose what they may have already acquired.

I trust these circumstances will bespeak the indulgence of the candid reader, for occasional inaccuracies of style and manner, from which I cannot presume to suppose this little work exempt.

Memoir

Lieutenant-Colonel Arthur Johnston was the eldest son of the late John Johnston, of Clare, in the County of Tyrone, Esq., whose ancestor (of the ancient house of Loverpay, a branch of the Annandale family) left Dumfriesshire in the beginning of the seventeenth century, and purchased considerable estates in the Counties of Tyrone and Fermanagh.

Colonel Johnston, the subject of this *Narrative*, was born in 1778, and when very young received his Ensign's and Lieutenant's commissions in the 19th Regiment, and accompanied that corps to Ceylon, where he early attracted the attention of the governor of the island, and was placed on his Staff.

His command of a detachment of his regiment to Kandy in 1804 is still spoken of in Ceylon with admiration. Major Forbes, in his work on Ceylon, recently published, makes frequent mention of it, and says—

> That the gallantry of Captain Johnston and his party taught the Kandians a respect for British troops which they had not felt before, and afterwards reluctantly admitted; and that one of the chiefs, who harassed Captain Johnston's retreat, assured *him* that the commander of that party must have been in alliance with supernatural powers. His personal escape while passing through such a continual ambush, and his superior judgment and energy, were unaccountable, unless this explanation were admitted.

His naturally fine constitution, however, never recovered the effects of that severe and trying expedition, and he was shortly obliged to return to Europe; soon after which, he joined the senior department of the Royal Military College at Wickham as student, and was selected by the *commandant* to act for him during his absence in Spain.

On the return of Sir Howard Douglass, he was made Assistant-Commandant—a situation which he held till the conclusion of the war; and when inquiries were started as to what retrenchment could be made in that department, he suggested that his appointment could better be dispensed with than many others.

He married Martha, eldest daughter of Thomas Smith, of Shalden, in Hampshire, Esq. He died and was buried at Shalden, in June, 1824.

Narrative of an Expedition to Candy

Before I enter on the detail of the operations of the detachment, which I had the honour to command on the expedition of 1804 against Candy, it may be proper to explain the peculiar nature of Candian warfare, and to describe the country and the character of the inhabitants, considered with relation to military affairs; since to these circumstances may be attributed, in a great measure, the want of success which in the interior of Ceylon has too frequently attended the operations of the regular troops of Europe against the undisciplined rabble by whom they have been opposed.

Ceylon, situated at the entrance of the Bay of Bengal, is reckoned about the size of Ireland. It consists of two great divisions; the one possessed by Europeans, the other exclusively occupied by the natives, and governed by the King of Candy. The part actually in possession of the English encircles, like a belt, the territories subject to the King of Candy, comprehending the whole coast of the island, in a circumference which varies from ten to twenty and thirty miles in breadth, its extent inland being regulated by the terms of various treaties concluded between the King of Candy and the successive European invaders of his territory, at the termination of their different wars. The residence of the English is confined to the principal settlements on the coast; the rest of their territory is inhabited and cultivated partly by Cingalese, and partly by Malabars; the former occupying the southern parts, and the latter the northern coast, adjacent to the continent of India, from whence they gradually migrated.

Our knowledge of the interior of Ceylon is still extremely imperfect. The ruggedness of the country, and the insalubrity of the climate at any distance from the coast, have hitherto prevented our obtaining an accurate survey even of those parts in the interior under our own immediate control. Of those in possession of the Candians, consisting principally of steep and lofty mountains, in many places covered with impenetrable forests, still less is known. Well aware that our ignorance of their passes and defiles forms one of the best safeguards of their independence, the rulers of the Candian nation take all possible care to prevent our acquiring information on this subject. They watch the ingress and egress of their territory with unremitting vigilance. This is the less difficult, as the access is by paths along which two men can seldom go abreast. In these paths gates are fixed, and guards stationed, to prevent the entrance of strangers, and to examine all passengers. Few Europeans, even in time of peace, venture to approach these barriers; and the continued detention of Major Davie, since the unfortunate fate of his detachment, notwithstanding the unwearied exertions of Governor North and General Maitland to effect his liberation, is an example of the extreme difficulty of escape.

It does not appear that the Portuguese and Dutch armies, which at different times penetrated the interior, were accompanied by men of science capable of taking topographical surveys of the country. Indeed, the officers who commanded those armies do not seem to have attached so much importance to this species of military knowledge as we now find it to deserve. They have not left us any general description of the country, nor even of those parts which were the scenes of their own operations. The accounts which remain of their campaigns abound, indeed, in details of battles and marches, describing the sufferings and privations of their troops, but convey no topographical information.

The government of Candy, like most Eastern governments, is purely despotic. The standing army consists of a few hundred men, chiefly mercenaries, who are generally stationed about the king's person. They are armed with muskets, taken at different times, or purchased from their European invaders. Although they possess little, if any, of what is considered discipline in Europe, yet the Candians have acquired, in their frequent conflicts with the Portuguese and Dutch, a considerable knowledge and dexterity in that species of warfare which is best suited to the nature of the country and the disposition of the inhabitants. Conscious of their inability to resist the regular attack of European troops, and aware of the advantages they possess in being familiar with the country and inured to the climate, they avoid close combat, preferring an irregular and desultory warfare. They harass the enemy in his march, hanging on his flanks, cutting off his supplies, interrupting the communication between his divisions, and occupying the heights which command the passes, from whence they fire in perfect security from behind rocks or trees. They aim principally at the *coolies*, who carry the ammunition and provisions, well knowing that, without these, a regular force can make but little progress.

To dislodge them from these heights is a task of extreme difficulty, as the paths leading to them are mostly on the opposite sides of the mountains, and only known to the inhabitants.

They are accustomed to impede the march of hostile troops by felling, and placing as abattis, large trees across the defiles. In narrow passes, where they cannot be avoided, this contrivance presents a most serious obstacle to the march of troops; for cutting up and removing a large tree is not the business of a moment.

One of their maxims is, seldom to press closely an enemy marching into their country; being certain that the diseases incident to Europeans in that climate, and the want of provisions, will soon oblige him to fall back; the farther he advances, the better he promotes their scheme of defence, as they can thus throw more numerous impediments in the way of his return. In the meantime, they are busily employed in blocking up the roads through which they think it most probable that he will attempt to retreat; when encumbered by a long train of sick and wounded, exhausted by fatigue and want of provisions, and probably destitute of ammunition (which frequently happens from desertion of the *coolies*), then it is, and then only, that they attack him, exerting all their energies and skill to harass and cut off his retreat.

What makes the situation of the troops, under those circumstances, still more distressing is, that every man who falls into the hands of the enemy is certain of immediate death. Nor does this inhuman practice arise from thirst of blood, or the gratification of revenge; it is a consequence of the reward offered by the King of Candy for the heads of his enemies, and of the desire of affording proofs of personal courage.

The Candians will even decapitate their own countrymen when killed in action, and carry the heads to their chiefs, as belonging to the enemy, in order to obtain this reward and distinction. I had frequent opportunities of ascertaining this fact. On surprising their posts at night, which we often effected without the loss of a man, and afterwards passing over the ground, we invariably found their slain without heads.

The nobles hold their lands by tenure of service, and are obliged, when called upon, to join the king at the head of a third of their vassals, should that number be required. This enables the king to dispense with a large regular force, which would be burthensome to his finances, and to bring into the field, on any emergency, a considerable portion of the male population of his kingdom.

Each village has its chief, with several inferior officers, in proportion to its size. The chief, on receiving an order from his *dessa*, or lord, summons every third, fourth, or fifth man, according to the nature of his instructions, and proceeds with his feudatory levies to the place of rendezvous. Each soldier is provided with a musket, and carries with him fifteen days' provisions, and a small cooking vessel. A few are armed with bows and arrows. A leaf of the *talipot* tree, an extensive umbrella, serves to protect him from the heat of the sun during the day, and two men, by placing the broad end of their leaves together, may form a tent that will completely defend them against the rains or dews, by night.

The provisions of the Candian are equally portable with his tent. Although, in most parts of the continent of India, rice forms the principal article of food amongst all ranks of natives, in Ceylon, and particularly in the interior of the island, it is reserved for the higher classes, and is a luxury of which the lowest order of the people seldom partake. The chief food of the poorer sort is a grain that grows on the hills, with little cultivation, and without watering. This, together with a root dug from the bottom of the tanks, and a decoction of the bark of a tree found in abundance in the forests, constitute their principal means of support. Men accustomed to such diet cannot be supposed to require many luxuries in the field. Two or three cocoanuts, a few cakes made of the grain I have just described, and a small quantity of rice, compose the whole of the soldier's stock for the campaign. His other wants he is certain of being always able to supply.

Thus equipped, the Candian soldier follows his chief, to whom he is accustomed to pay the most implicit obedience. He crawls through the paths in the woods, for the purpose of commanding the roads through which the hostile troops must pass, or climbs the mountains, and places himself behind a rock, or a tree, patiently to await the enemy's approach. At the end of fifteen days he is relieved by a fresh requisition from the village; and thus the army is constantly supplied with fresh troops, totally unencumbered, the party relieved always carrying home their sick and wounded companions. Another great advantage attending this system of warfare is, that the soldier will more cheerfully encounter fatigues and privations, which he knows are to be of short continuance, and must terminate at a certain fixed period. He

20

is also supported by the hope of shortly returning to his village, and recounting his exploits.

Such a system could only answer in a country like that which I have been describing, where the theatre of war is almost always within certain limits, so that whatever be the fortune of the contest, the soldier is seldom removed above two, and never more than four days' march from his own abode.

Nor is it necessary to furnish those returning home with escorts, as they have little to fear from the slow and unwieldy movements of their European enemies, whom they can at all times avoid by taking a circuitous route. A Candian army, thus unencumbered by sick and baggage, and being perfect masters of their intricate paths and passes, is enabled to move with much more rapidity than regular troops, strangers to the country, and encumbered, as they usually are, with artillery, ammunition, baggage, provisions, and frequently a long train of sick and wounded, can possibly do.

The climate also, which, as in every uncultivated country, is unfavourable to the constitutions of its invaders, has been a powerful auxiliary of the Candians, in all their wars with the European powers, who have successively had possession of the maritime parts of the island.

The Portuguese were the first Europeans who obtained a footing in Ceylon. They occupied a considerable portion of the island from 1517 to 1658, a period of 141 years. They at first came as merchants, and obtained permission from the king to erect a small factory at Colombo, which, however, they soon converted into a fort. The spirit of conquest which then animated the Portuguese nation would not allow them to remain long contented with what they had thus peaceably obtained. They made gradual encroachments on the adjacent territories; and being strengthened by reinforcements from their other settlements in India, they not only threw off all appearance of restraint and allegiance to the prince, but even carried the war into the heart of his country. The situation of the island, divided into several governments, each jealous of the other, was particularly favourable to their views.

By the superiority of their arms they soon extended their conquests over some of the most valuable provinces, and by their address and insinuating manners obtained a degree of influence at the court of Candy, which none of their successors have ever been able to acquire. They even persuaded one of the Emperors of Ceylon, at his death, in 1597, to bequeath his kingdom to the King of Portugal: a bequest which was attended with no permanent advantage, and only involved them in fresh wars.

The Portuguese Government in Ceylon appears to have committed a great error in policy, in raising the Cingalese to the rank of generals, and entrusting them with the command of armies. At one time, four of these persons, under the title of *Modiliars*, went over to the enemy, by a preconcerted arrangement, which occasioned the destruction of the Portuguese general, Constantin de Sâa, and of his whole army.

Ribeiro, a Portuguese captain, in his *History of Ceylon*, a work of authenticity, but now very scarce, gives an account of the whole affair; which he thus prefaces:—

> We had four *Modiliars* in our armies, *viz.*, Don Alexis, Don Balthasar, Don Casmus, and Don Theodosius. As they were all four born at Colombo, of the Christian faith, very rich, and allied to the first families of the island, they were made commanders of armies. The general had much consideration for them, had them always with him, admitted them frequently to his councils, and very often followed their advice. Notwithstanding, although they had considerable establishments amongst us, and were under great obligations to the general, they did not scruple to enter into a secret treaty with the King of Candy, which, as shall be seen, was the cause of our total ruin.—Ribeiro *Hist. of Ceylon,* lib. ii. cap. 1.

This treaty had been carrying on for three years, at the end of which time, things appearing now to be ripe for their purposes, the *Modiliars* persuaded the general, that the honour of Portugal required that the King of Candy should be chastised for conduct which they represented as insulting to the Portuguese crown. These *Modiliars* commanded the advanced guard of the Portuguese army, composed of 20,000 native soldiers. As the hostile armies approached each other, Casmus, one of the principal traitors, by way of signal, struck off the head of a Portuguese, and displayed it on the point of his lance; on which the three others declared themselves, and their example was followed by all the native troops of the army. The general, and the European soldiers, consisting of only 1500 men, after an obstinate defence, were at length overpowered, and annihilated.

This event contributed principally to effect the ruin, and ultimately the expulsion of the Portuguese nation from Ceylon.

I have introduced this circumstance, in order to guard my countrymen from ever reposing an unlimited confidence in the natives of Ceylon. The Cingalese, however heartily they may appear to enter into our views, are, notwithstanding, a very venal and treacherous people. That four men, enjoying a rank and emoluments next to the governor, and superior to any which they could possess in the Candian country, should have thus gone over to the enemy, is a proof how little able they are to resist the temptation of a bribe; and it does not appear that their character has since that period undergone, in this respect, any material change. Although it is not likely that the *Modiliars* should ever be entrusted with any high military command under the British Government, yet they may have opportunities, in other situations, if admitted into our confidence, of betraying our plans to the enemy. As from their knowledge of the country, and their influence with the natives, whom we employ as *coolies*, they must necessarily be much about the persons of the officers commanding detachments of our armies in the interior; it is necessary that while we make use of them in their various situations, we should, as much as possible, prevent their penetrating into our designs.

In 1658, the Portuguese were finally expelled from Ceylon by the Dutch, in alliance with the Cingalese. The Dutch, when they found themselves in possession of those ports along the coast, which had formerly been occupied by the Portuguese, soon threw off the mask of moderation, which they had till then worn; and war, as might be expected, ensued between them and the King of Candy. Although the Dutch at the time possessed great resources in India, and their troops were not inferior to any in Europe, they could effect but little against the natives, defended by the climate and the nature of the country.

The flower of their armies either fell victims to disease, or were cut off in skirmishes with the enemy, whilst the loss of the Candians was comparatively trifling. The constitutions of the Portuguese, from the nature of their own climate, and the simplicity of their diet, were better suited to the country than those of the Dutch, and rendered them more fit to undergo the fatigues and privations of Candian warfare. They also assimilated their manners more to those of the native Indians, which, above every thing, contributed to their successes.

On the other hand, the haughty republican manners of the Dutch were not so well adapted to the Indian character. Inflated by national pride, they despised customs and prejudices, which appeared to them absurd, only perhaps because they differed from their own. To disgust their friends, and increase the number and resources of their enemies, was the natural result of such impolitic conduct. Soldiers, and particularly officers, ought to recollect, that advantages gained in the field by the blood and valour of their countrymen may frequently be rendered useless by a foolish display of national pride, by a cold and repulsive behaviour towards the natives, or an ill-timed manifestation of contempt for their customs and prejudices.

The Dutch, however, were enabled, after successive conflicts during a series of years, in which thousands of their countrymen perished, to complete the belt that now encircles the King of Candy's territories, and wholly to exclude him from the sea-coast.

Their last war of any importance was in 1763, when they attacked Candy with an army of upwards of 8,000 men, composed of Europeans, *sepoys* from their possessions on the coasts of Coromandel and Malabar, and Malays from Batavia. The latter are more dreaded by the natives even than European troops. The Dutch, with little opposition, got possession of the enemy's capital, in which they maintained themselves for upwards of nine months, with the loss of nearly half their force. After having suffered almost every privation, their provisions being nearly exhausted, and all communication with their settlements on the coast cut off for three months, the officer on whom the command had devolved (Major Frankana), who appears to have done everything that could be expected from a brave and experienced officer, called a council of war, in which it was determined, after much debating, as the only means of preserving the wreck of the army from utter destruction, immediately to abandon the place, and to force their way to Columbo.

The army was pursued by the Candians, who, fortunately not being aware of the intended retreat, had not time to block up the roads. They, however, harassed them by every means in their power, and instantly put to death those who had the misfortune to drop in the rear.

The invalids, who were unable to keep up with the line, were collected in churches by the commanding officer of the retreating army, and labels imploring for mercy were in vain placed round their necks. The moment the Candians came up with them, they were cruelly butchered. The survivors at length reached Columbo, exhausted with hunger and fatigue.

In 1796 the Dutch, after having been in possession of the country 143 years, were in their turn expelled by the English, aided by the

Candians, whose policy it is invariably to join the invading army.

That the dangers and difficulties of war in Candy have by no means diminished since Ceylon fell into our hands, will hereafter fully appear from the mode of conducting our expeditions, and their unfavourable results. The want of supplies in the interior renders it indispensable for an invading army to carry provisions, as well as stores, along with it. The carriage of *doolies*, or litters for the sick and wounded, and camp equipage, also requires the addition of an almost incredible number of followers. It has been found that, at the lowest computation, a detachment properly equipped requires, even for the short period of fifteen days, at the rate of four *coolies* for each soldier; so that, for a detachment of 600 men, the followers alone will amount to 2,400, requiring daily provision for 3,000 mouths.

The *coolies* have the utmost aversion to a Candian campaign; to collect any number of them is consequently attended with difficulties and delay, and it can only be done by pressing. The instant it is known in any of the districts that the native chief has received orders to seize, as they not improperly term it, a certain number of *coolies*, the villages are deserted by the lower class of the inhabitants, who, to avoid the police-officers, either conceal themselves in the forests, or take refuge in the Candian territories. After considerable delays, the chief seldom succeeds in procuring above half the number required; and thus the advantages which we seem at first sight to enjoy over the enemy, of having always a considerable disciplined force, ready to march at a moment's notice, are completely lost, from the impossibility of any prompt movement.

By the flight of the *coolies*, intimation of our design is soon conveyed to the Candian Government, and the necessary orders immediately issued for calling out the inhabitants, which orders are punctually complied with, as well from the dread of the punishment of disobedience, as from the people being interested in the defence of their country. Long before our detachments can be equipped, the enemy is arrayed in force ready to receive them.

The aversion of the natives to serve as *coolies* in our armies is founded on very obvious reasons. The burdens which they are obliged to carry are heavy, and their progress consequently slow. They are frequently exposed to a galling fire, doubtful of being taken care of, if wounded, and certain of being put to death if made prisoners; their post is more dangerous than that of the fighting part of the army; while they are not, like the soldiers, buoyed up by the prospect of any military advantage or preferment, or excited by the stimulus of fame.

It cannot, therefore, be surprising that the Cingalese, naturally timid, and rendered indolent by their climate and mode of living, should use every effort in their power to avoid being impressed on such a service, or that they should, when forced into it, afterwards desert. This is a frequent occurrence, and is often attended with serious consequences. They are also apt, without any intention of escaping from the army, when unexpectedly attacked, from the mere impulse of fear, to throw down their loads, and rush into the woods to conceal themselves. This is a practice which neither threats nor entreaties can check; but their design being simply to elude the danger of the moment, their head man generally succeeds in rallying them as soon as the firing ceases. This dispersion of the *coolies* for a time entirely stops the line of march, as it would be impossible to move forward without them, but by abandoning the sick, the wounded, and the stores to the enemy.

These disasters happen mostly in defiles; and the enemy, well knowing the disposition of our *coolies*, generally selects such places for attacking them.

All these difficulties were unhappily exemplified in the marches of our troops during the Candian war. In the year 1802, a wanton act of violence on the part of the Candians, for which reparation was in vain demanded, terminated in open hostility between the two governments. Without any pretence of aggression, our merchants, in carrying on their trade in the Candian territory, had been attacked, and plundered of considerable property. After repeated remonstrances on the part of the British Government against this outrage, and evasive delays and violated promises on the part of the Candians, Mr. North felt himself under the painful necessity of proceeding to hostile measures.

On the 31st of January, 1803, a division of our forces, under the command of General Macdowal, composed of the flower of the Ceylon Army, began their march from Columbo, and after suffering much delay from want of *coolies*, entered the enemy's territory on the 6th of February. On the 20th, in the neighbourhood of Candy, they formed a junction with the division of Colonel Barbut, which had marched about the same time from Trincomalé. Their united force amounted to 3,000 soldiers; and, as usual, they met with little opposition from the Candians in their advance.

On the following morning the troops crossed the great Candian river, Mahavilla Gonga, and took possession of the capital of Candy, which was totally deserted by its inhabitants on their approach. Not an individual was found in the place; and almost every article of value had been removed to the mountains. The possession of the capital, which, in most countries, would be considered as an object of great importance, if not decisive of the conquest, here afforded no advantages whatever to the captors.

Temporary works were thrown up, under the direction of our engineers, to defend it from any attack of the natives during the approaching monsoon; and some attempts were made to collect provisions for the garrison from the surrounding country. And, owing to the exertions of Captain Madge, of the 19th regiment (whom Colonel Barbut had appointed to the command of Fort Macdowal, a post situated about sixteen miles from Candy, on the Trincomalé road), considerable quantities of grain were from time to time collected, and forwarded to Candy for the use of the garrison. These, however, were measures attended with extreme difficulty; our foraging parties being constantly harassed by the enemy: insomuch that it had at length become necessary to procure all our supplies from Columbo. But sickness and desertion among the *coolies*, and the difficulty of escorting them through an enemy's country, where they were continually harassed, rendered this mode of supply extremely precarious and insufficient.

About the middle of March, the rains set in, which rendered the conveyance of farther supplies from the coast nearly impracticable. It was, therefore, judged advisable to withdraw all the troops from the interior that could prudently be spared. Accordingly, in the beginning of April the main body of the forces marched from the Candian territory towards Columbo and Trincomalé, leaving 1,000 soldiers, consisting of Europeans and natives, under the command of Colonel Barbut, for the defence of Candy.

A truce having been concluded between General Macdowal and the *Adigar* (prime minister of the Candians), and the fortifications being finished, this force was deemed sufficient for any probable contingency.

Before the departure of the General, Mooto Sawmy, whom the English Government supported in his claims on the throne of Candy, was crowned in the palace with all the forms of Eastern ceremonial. But not one of the Candians appeared to support his pretensions. This prince entered into a treaty with the English to whom, amongst other valuable concessions, he ceded the province of the seven Corles.

As soon as the enemy found that a considerable part of the forces had been withdrawn, and that those left behind began to suffer from the effects of climate, they made preparation for a general attack on Candy, which, notwithstanding the truce, they invested on the 23rd of June, and the state of the garrison was such as to induce Major Davie, who had succeeded to the command on the death of Colonel Barbut, to surrender the town the next day, on condition of being allowed to march with his garrison to Trincomalé, and that the sick and wounded should be taken care of by the Candian Government.

On their arrival on the banks of the river, about three miles from the town, they found it not fordable, and applied to the Candians to assist them with rafts to convey the troops across. This request was apparently assented to; but for two days, under various pretences, compliance with it was continually evaded.

In the meantime the Candians, in violation of the articles of capitulation, in which Mooto Sawmy had been included, demanded the person of that unfortunate prince, as the only condition on which the detachment would be permitted to cross the river. To this Major Davie, having assurances from the king that Mooto Sawmy should be kindly treated, after much hesitation, agreed. This unhappy prince was led back to the capital, where, with two of his relatives, he was immediately put to death, and all his followers shockingly mutilated.

No sooner was this concession made, than the Candians demanded that the troops should deliver up their arms. This also was agreed to. The native troops were then immediately separated from the Europeans; and the latter were led out, officers and soldiers, in pairs, and with a few exceptions perfidiously massacred.

Whilst these horrid acts were perpetrating on the banks of the river, a scene no less revolting to humanity was passing in the capital. All the sick in Candy, to the amount of 120 men, were murdered in cold blood, as they lay, incapable of resistance, in the hospital.

Of all this ill-fated detachment, Major Davie, Captains Rumley and Humphreys, and Corporal Barnsley, of the 19th, alone survived the dreadful catastrophe. The three former were detained in the hands of the Candians; and the latter, after having been severely wounded, and considered by the enemy as dead, contrived to escape to Fort Macdowal during the night. This post, as has been before-mentioned, was commanded by Captain Madge, of the 19th regiment, who had for three days been closely besieged, and completely surrounded.

Repeated offers had been made to him of a passport to Trincomalé with the whole of his sick and baggage, on condition of surrendering the place, which, of course, had been indignantly rejected; and on Barnsley's approach to the post, the enemy, with their characteristic cunning, sent him forward with a flag of truce, in the hope that his communication of the capture of Candy would show the uselessness of any further resistance, and produce the surrender of the fort. (Barnsley's Deposition.—See Appendix.)

Captain Madge, however, finding himself in the midst of the enemy's country, unsupported and without provisions, immediately determined to force a retreat to Trincomalé, a distance of 126 miles, before the Candians, who were celebrating their recent successes in the capital, could bring the whole of their troops against him, or indeed could be aware of his intentions. His party consisted of 14 Europeans and about 70 Malays, of whom the whole of the former were sick, and a considerable number of the latter incapable of much exertion; with this handful of men, under circumstances so discouraging, he commenced his arduous march on the 27th of June, at night; and though surrounded by large bodies of the enemy, who were continually harassing and keeping up a severe fire on his flanks and rear, he nevertheless succeeded in reaching Trincomalé on the 3rd of July, after suffering many privations and distresses.

Indeed the promptitude with which this retreat was attempted, and the skill and courage with which it was effected, and a part of our brave troops rescued from the sad fate of their devoted associates, reflects the highest credit on the military talents of Captain Madge, and was distinguished by the most marked approbation of government, and also the commander of the forces.

The other posts which had been established in the interior fell successively into the hands of the enemy.

The fate of the troops that occupied the two small posts of Ghirriagamme and Gallighederah, in the neighbourhood of Candy, was never ascertained.

The post of Dambadinia, situated about 60 miles from Candy, on the Columbo road, was garrisoned only by a few invalids, under the command of Ensign Grant, who had often distinguished himself by his gallantry and activity during the war. On the 26th of June he was joined by Lieutenant Nixon, of the 19th, with a few invalids, who had left Candy during the truce, when the command devolved upon this latter officer. On the 29th they were attacked by the Candians in great force, many of whom were dressed in the uniform of the soldiers killed in Candy. Although sheltered only by temporary breastworks, in some places composed merely of rice-bags, Lieutenant Nixon and his little party stoutly defended themselves, repulsing the enemy in repeated assaults. The Candians several times offered the most flattering terms of capitulation, which were no less gallantly than judiciously rejected; and on the 2nd of July the garrison was brought off by a body of troops from Columbo, under the command of Capt. Blackall, of the 51st regiment.

Thus fell the last of our posts in the Candian country, and in the course of ten days from the retaking of the capital not an inch of ground remained to us beyond our original frontier.

Thus defended by their climate, their mountains, and their forests, the Candians, by adhering steadily to the same mode of warfare, have been enabled to resist the incursions of their several European invaders for three centuries. Although successively attacked by the Portuguese, Dutch, and English, when in the zenith of their eastern conquests, and repeatedly driven from their capital, they are now in as complete possession of the interior of their country, and govern it as independently of any European influence, as at any period of their history since the first invasion of their coast.

The Candians, flushed with their successes, and knowing that our forts on the coast were now weakly garrisoned, poured down from their mountains in the months of August and September, in the hope of utterly expelling us from the island. And in this attempt they were joined by the native inhabitants of our own settlements, who rose, as of one accord, to accelerate our expulsion. This fact affords a strong and convincing proof that, when we lose the power of the sword, to entertain any hope of preserving India through the affection of the natives, would be building on the most unstable foundation. So strong is their attachment to their ancient governments, laws, language, manners, and religious opinions, that three centuries of European domination have not diminished its force. But in leaving their fastnesses, the Candians relinquished those advantages which alone made them formidable; and reinforcements arriving most seasonably to our army from the Cape of Good Hope and Bengal, their efforts were completely defeated.

The government, thus strengthened, considered itself in a situation to retaliate on the enemy; and detachments entered the country from various points, laying it waste wherever they penetrated.

This mode of warfare, however repugnant to the feelings of government, appeared the only one now left us to pursue; and while it contributed to the security of our own districts from invasion, it held out a hope that, by convincing the King of Candy of his inability to protect his people, he might ultimately be led to a negotiation for peace.

However, in August, 1804, being still further strengthened by the arrival of the 65th regiment from Europe, and considerable reinforcements from Madras and Bengal, it was resolved once more to penetrate into the interior, and to take possession of the enemy's capital.

Great difficulties having been experienced in procuring a sufficient number of *coolies* to accompany the forces from Columbo and Trincomalé, under the command of General Macdowal and Lieut.-Colonel Barbut, in 1803, it was now thought advisable, from the magnitude of the army about to be employed, to divide it into six columns, which should march separately from different stations, so as to meet at a given time at one central point, in the vicinity of the capital. The following settlements, *viz.*:—Columbo, Negumbo,[1] Chilou, Poutelam, Hambingtotte, Batticolo, and Trincomalé, were the points from whence the detachments were to proceed.

It was hoped that, by this means, each division would be enabled to procure a sufficient number of *coolies* for its own immediate wants in the district from which it was to march; whereas it would have been almost impossible to collect, in any reasonable time, from different parts of the island, a sufficient number for two very large detachments. This mode of attack, it was expected, would disconcert the enemy, and lead to information relative to the interior of the island, hitherto so little explored by Europeans.

General Wemyss, who had succeeded General Macdowal in the command of the forces, desirous of ascertaining, by personal inspection, the state of the detachments at the different stations, and of inquiring into the practicability and eligibility of the different routes, determined, in the month of August, 1804, to make a tour of the island. On visiting Batticolo, where I then commanded, he explained to me (as one of those selected to conduct a detachment) the meditated expedition, and his views respecting the combined attack on Candy. From Batticolo the General proceeded to Trincomalé, from whence I shortly afterwards received the following letter, dated Sept. 3, 1804:—

---

1. The troops from Negumbo and Chilou were to have been united: consequently would have formed but one detachment.

(Most Secret.)

Trincomalé, Sept. 3, 1804.

Sir,

In the event of your not having marched towards Arriagam, you are directed to have a strong detachment in perfect readiness, as soon as possible, to march to Candy, by the route of Ouva. To enable you to equip a strong force, a detachment of Europeans and natives will march from this as soon as the weather clears; and, when joined by it, you will proceed towards the enemy's country, arranging so as to be within eight days' march of the town of Candy on the 20th instant, which is the day fixed for the commencement of general co-operations. You will then proceed direct upon Candy, not doing any injury to the country or people, unless opposed; and as different detachments are ordered to march precisely on the 20th for general co-operation for the destruction of the enemy's capital, the various columns will be put in motion from Columbo, Hambingtotte, Trincomalé, Negumbo, Chilou, and Pouttalim, the whole to be within eight days' march of Candy on the 20th instant; and, on the 28th or 29th, the commander of the forces fully expects a general junction on the heights of Candy.

The general fully relies on the execution of these instructions; and, from your well-known zeal and activity, he has no doubt of a perfect completion of his wishes.

I have the honour to be,

Sir,

Your obedient servant,

R. Mowbray,

Act. D. Adj.-Gen.

Immediately on the receipt of this letter I made the necessary preparations for our march.

Previous to entering on a detail of the operations of the detachment which I had the honour to command, it may be proper to offer a few remarks relative to the district of Batticolo. This district is situated on the south-east side of the island, and is the most remote from the seat of government of all our possessions in Ceylon. The fort is built on a broad river of the same name, navigable for small vessels, and about four miles from the coast. Our territory here extends from fifteen to twenty miles up the country, and continues low and flat, as far as the Candian frontier, which is formed by a chain of steep and lofty mountains. Speaking of this part of the country, I shall avail myself of the beautifully descriptive language of the Rev. Mr. Cordiner, in his *History of Ceylon*:—

> The south-east coast, viewed from the sea, is particularly picturesque and romantic. The country, in the highest degree mountainous, presents hills beyond hills, many beautiful and verdant, others huge and rocky, of extraordinary shapes, resembling ruined battlements, ancient castles, and lofty pyramids.

Of these mountains we have little knowledge. The natives represent them as covered with immense forests, the northern parts of which are inhabited by the Vedas, or Bedas, a singular and savage tribe, nearly in a state of nature, and who hold no intercourse with the other inhabitants of the country. They are by many considered as the aborigines of the island.

Beyond this chain, and to the southward, are the still more rugged mountains of Ouva, celebrated for the secure asylum they afford to the kings of Candy, when driven from their capital. It was here that, in 1631, the whole Portuguese Army, with their general, Constantin de Sáa, in attempting to pursue the King in his retreat, were, in consequence of the defection of the *Modiliars,* overpowered, and perished to a man. The small-pox had of late depopulated a great part of the district of Batticolo; those who were not themselves affected with the malady (from the dread entertained by the natives of India of this dangerous disease), deserted those who were, flying, to avoid contagion, to the woods. This, together with the general disaffection of the natives to our cause, rendered it impossible to procure above half the number of *coolies* required for the use of the detachment. I was therefore obliged to supply the deficiency by carriage bullocks, a circumstance which afterwards occasioned considerable embarrassment and delay.

On the 14th of September I received a letter from the acting adjutant-general, dated at Jaffnapatam, the 8th of the same month, of which the following is a copy:—

To Capt. Johnson, Commanding Batticolo.

Sir,
The Commander of the Forces directs you will, on the receipt of this, reduce your division to 300 men, as you will then be enabled to have a sufficiency of *coolies* for the purpose of entering the enemy's dominions. As some unforeseen obstacles have

prevented the various columns forming the intended junction, about the 28th or 29th instant, on the heights of Candy, agreeably to the instructions transmitted to you on the 3rd instant, you are directed to march on the 20th of this month, bending your course towards the province of Ouva, and form junction at the entrance of that part with the detachment ordered from Hambingtotte, which will march the same day, the 20th instant, by the route of Catragame, on the great road leading to Candy, which is frequented by the king, for visiting that temple.

You will, in junction with the other detachments, concert such measures as will best tend to effect the greatest devastation and injury to the enemy's country.

All persons found in arms to be immediately made examples of, and the peaceful and defenceless peasant to be spared.

You will note in writing all observations relative to the country, as our future operations will be guided by them in that part, and transmit your journal to me, for the general's information.

I have the honour to be, &c.

    (Signed)   R. Mowbray, Act. D. Adj.-Gen.

Jaffnapatam,
8th Sept. 1804.

Considering this letter as merely a modification of the original plan of operations, as far as related to *change of route and day of march*, I immediately sent off an express to Colonel Maddison, commandant of the Hambingtotte detachment, naming a place for the junction of our columns. The distance from Batticolo to Hambingtotte being nearly 200 miles, and our orders being to commence our march on the 20th, it would have been impossible to receive Colonel Maddison's answer to my dispatch before that period. Of course there could be no room for mutual consultation, in regard to the place of junction; it was indispensable, therefore, that I should specify it at once, and I accordingly named Kiratavillé, a large village situated on the frontiers of Ouva, the residence of a Candian chief, and likely in consequence to be well-known to the guides.

The remainder of the narrative will be most properly continued, and best understood, in the form of a journal.

Sept. 20.—In the evening embarked with the British troops and stores, on the Batticolo river, and proceeded, during the night, to Surcamony, a village on its banks, distant 27 miles.

21.—This day principally occupied in landing the stores. Joined by the native troops, who had proceeded by land from Batticolo.

Our detachment now consisted of the following numbers:—

	EUROPEANS.						NATIVES.					
—	Captains.	Lieutenant.	Ensign.	Serjeants.	Drummers.	Privates.	Subidar, or Capt.	Jemidar, or Lieut.	Hav. or Serjeant.	Drummers.	Privates.	Grand Total.
Royal Artillery				1		6						7
His Majesty's 19th Regiment	2			3	1	64						70
———— Malay ditto	1						1	1	4		46	53
1st Batt. Bengal Volunteers	1							1	9	2	75	88
2nd do. ditto ...	2						1	1	5	2	76	87
(Pioneers and Coolies 550).	6			4	1	70	2	3	18	4	197	305

N.B.   One one-pounder, and one 4½ cohorn.

Sept. 22.—Marched at daylight to the westward, keeping in a southerly direction as much as the nature of the country would admit, in order to approximate the route of Colonel Maddison's detachment.

23, 24, 25, 26.—Followed the same course, expecting, as we drew nearer to the place of rendezvous, to hear of the Hambingtotte division.

27.—Reached Sambapelly after a very fatiguing march of above seventy miles (from Surcamony), over a country wild and mountainous in the highest degree. During the last sixty miles we had not seen a house or a human being, nor was there anything except the paths through the forests and round the bases of the mountains, to induce a belief that this quarter had ever been peopled. We crossed one broad river, and several smaller streams, none of which fortunately impeded our march. The weather during the day was close and sultry, the circulation of the air being impeded by the forests; the nights, on the contrary, were foggy and cold.

These changes of climate began to take effect on the troops, and I found it necessary to send back from hence two Malays and twenty-two Bengal *sepoys*, who were indisposed. Sambapelly is a small village, near which stands the residence of a Candian chief. The country in the vicinity assumes a more favourable appearance. Some villages are discernible, and the valleys are in many parts cultivated.

28.—Marched at daylight, the country continuing mountainous, but the slopes of the hills in many places cleared, and the valleys in general cultivated. Passed through some villages, which were entirely deserted. Numerous parties of the enemy were seen at a distance, along the sides of the mountains, watching our movements, by which they seemed to be directed. About three o'clock, as the advanced guard was descending into a deep valley, close to the village of Kieratavally, they were fired upon by a party of the enemy, posted on the opposite hills, who fled as soon as they had discharged their pieces. Luckily one man, who was wounded, fell into our hands. Although we had now marched 124 miles from Batticolo, this was the first native to whom we had been enabled to speak.

It was here that I expected to meet the Hambingtotte division, but our prisoner had heard nothing of it, nor of any detachment than that under my command; a circumstance which, cut off as I was from communication by the surrounding enemy, created considerable anxiety. As it was impossible to remain stationary with a corps in a country where there was no possibility of procuring provisions of any kind, every article of that description having been removed to the mountains, and as I conceived there could be no doubt of the Hambingtotte division bringing up the rear, I lost no time in advancing, and the more so as I expected I must soon meet some of the other columns, which I imagined must shortly be concentrating themselves towards the capital. During the night we heard the shouts of the enemy, and saw their numerous fires in various directions along the sides of the mountains.

Kieratavally is a neat Candian village, situated in a well-cultivated part of the country. Before leaving it I set fire to a large house belonging to the Dessauve, that the Hambingtotte division on arriving there might see that we had already passed.

29.—Continued our route at daylight in the direction of Candy, anxiously looking out for other detachments of our troops. After marching sixteen miles over a country similar to what we had lately traversed, reached Pangaram, a large village, inhabited chiefly by Lubbies (a trading caste), and situated on the banks of the great river which passes Candy, and which is here about 150 yards broad. The village was, as usual, entirely deserted. The river being much swollen, we immediately began to prepare rafts. During the day the enemy hung on our flanks in considerable numbers, but did not oppose our progress otherwise than by exchanging a few shots with our advanced and rear guards. Towards night, however, they lined the opposite bank of the river, and seemed resolved to dispute the passage.

30.—The river having fallen considerably during the night, the enemy fled from the opposite bank, after a few discharges of round shot. A few volunteers made good their passage, and the river continuing to fall, the rest of our men were enabled to ford it. The stores were carried over on rafts. While this was going on, I detached Lieutenant Virgo, with a party of about sixty men, to destroy a palace of the King of Candy, situated seven miles down the river, in which I understood was a *depôt* of arms and military stores. They completely effected their object.

Oct. 1.—Continued our march towards Candy, and encamped in the evening in a small plain called Catavilly, distant fifteen miles from Pangaram. The country showed less appearance of cultivation. The enemy continued to hang on our flanks, firing now and then a few shots, but making no serious resistance.

2.—After marching eight miles, reached the ford of Padrapelly, where we crossed for the second time the Candian river, the course of which is very circuitous. Our passage was attended with great difficulty, owing to the rapidity of the stream, and the rockiness of the bottom. During the last two days, our path was extremely rugged, lying along the banks of the river, where the hills ended in high and shelving rocks, the soil being washed away by torrents. Encamped on the opposite bank, in a small opening, where we could procure no forage for our bullocks.

3.—Marched at daylight. During this morning the enemy seemed disposed to close with us; they killed a soldier of the 19th, and wounded some followers. After marching about eight miles, we began ascending the pass of Ourané, which we found steep, rocky, and intersected by deep ravines. About half way up we halted in the plain of Ourané, where we found plenty of excellent water, a most welcome refreshment to our men, who were exhausted by climbing up the mountains under the rays of a vertical sun, reflected from rocks, which, as the day advanced, became more and more heated. Meantime the enemy assembled in considerable numbers higher up the mountain, but were dislodged by Lieutenant Virgo, whom I had sent forward to secure the pass. Late in the evening we reached the summit, after a painful march of fourteen miles, and halted in a small village called Comanatavillé.

4.—The road on this day's march was worse than any we had yet passed; it lay along the brow of a mountain, in several places nearly perpendicular, where a false step would have caused a fall of several hundred feet. Being very narrow, many of the bullocks tumbled head-long down, and the path would have been altogether impracticable for these animals, had they not been habituated to carry merchandize along the hills. Here and there, where the earth had been washed away, or a rock fallen down, the natives had driven stakes horizontally into the sides of the mountain, forming a kind of bridge, over which travellers could pass. Had these given way under any of the men, they must have been dashed to pieces; or had they been previously re-moved, the hill would have been rendered impassable. This is one of the paths through which the King of Candy retreats to Ouva, when he is obliged to fly from his capital.

That the enemy should have forborne to check our advance by de-stroying the paths, can be accounted for only by supposing, that they thought it unlikely so small a force could push forward to the capital, and were in hourly expectation of our retreat by the same road, which I afterwards understood they had rendered impassable; or, unless, as is more likely, they wished, in compliance with their favourite system, to draw us into the heart of the country, and attack us when enfeebled by sickness and skirmishes.

We encamped, late in the evening, in a paddy (rice) field on the bank of the river, under a steep hill, which was occupied by the 3rd company of Bengal *sepoys*, under Lieutenant Povelary.

5.—At daylight the enemy covered the opposite bank, and opened a fire of musketry and *gengals* (Candian field-pieces) on our camp; but as it was situated in a hollow, most of the shot passed over our heads; two *sepoys*, however, were killed, and several *sepoys* and *coolies* wounded, and the tents much injured. The enemy attacked the hill above the camp, but were repulsed by Lieutenant Povelary with con-siderable loss. Our position was, notwithstanding, much exposed, both when in camp, and when prosecuting our march. On the right ran the river, nowhere fordable, and lined on its opposite bank by the enemy; on the left was a steep mountain, confining our march to the vicinity of the river. Our flankers on the left, it is true, occupied the summit of the mountain, and could, by a lateral movement, prevent our being galled from that side.

We began our march at nine a.m., our flankers on the right firing across the river on the enemy; but, as they were chiefly concealed behind rocks and trees, with little effect. The most distressing circumstance however was, that many of the bullocks, unaccustomed to the appearance of Europeans and to heavy firing, became wild and unmanageable, broke from their drivers, cast off their loads, and, rushing among the *coolies*, created much confusion and delay.

Having advanced about three miles in this state, we approached a large house standing nearly across the road, and about a hundred yards distant from the river. This house was filled with the enemy, who fired on the head of our column from holes pierced in the walls. Exactly opposite, on the other side of the river, I perceived a battery with one heavy gun (which I afterwards found to be a Dutch iron eight-pounder), and several *gengals* ready to open on us whenever we came within range. This made it necessary for me to pause: our loss had already been considerable; our troops, as well as *coolies*, were falling fast. To attempt to pass the battery with so lengthened a column as ours, disordered as it was by the confusion that had been occasioned by the bullocks, would have been highly imprudent, especially as our only field-piece upset at this time, by which the axletree of the carriage was broken; I therefore determined to storm the house, and, when in possession of it, to construct rafts for the purpose of passing the river and carrying the battery.

Our vanguard accordingly drove the enemy from the house, which we entered, and finding plenty of room for our whole corps, were enabled to dress the wounded and replace the axletree of our gun-carriage. We passed the remainder of the day in constructing a large raft of such materials as could be procured. Before Lieutenant Povelary, who flanked our left, could get possession of a high hill immediately above the house, the enemy were enabled to fire a volley through the roof, by which a bombardier of the Royal Artillery (Malcolm Campbell) was unfortunately killed. Though only a non-commissioned officer, his loss was severely felt by our small party, having rendered himself particularly useful by his exertions in getting the stores up the mountains during the march. The enemy's fire was now wholly directed against the house. They had luckily but little round shot for the large gun, and the grape and fire of the *gengals* did no material injury.

The night presented a scene different from what we had yet witnessed. On the opposite bank and the adjoining hills were thousands of the enemy, every fourth or fifth man carrying a *choulou* or torch. At intervals, a shout of exultation was set up from the battery in our front, which was repeated by those around, and re-echoed by others on the neighbouring hills. The object of this was to terrify our native troops, and induce them to desert.

During the night, the enemy contrived to turn aside a stream, which passed close to the house, and had supplied us with water the day before; after which we could not procure any, even for the sick and wounded. I here endeavoured, but with little effect, to use the *coehorn*.

Owing to the wretched state of the fuzees nineteen shells out of twenty-three thrown into the enemy's work fell dead, although these shells had been sent us for service from Trincomalé a few days only before we set out.

6.—Our spirits were greatly raised this morning by a report from that active and zealous officer, Lieutenant Povelary, who occupied the hill above the house, stating that he heard distinctly a heavy firing in the neighbourhood of Candy. This I concluded must be some of our detachments crossing the river at Wattapalogo or Kattagastoly. About seven a.m., after much labour and loss, we carried our raft to the river, which sunk as soon as a couple of soldiers got upon it, being composed of iron wood, the only material within our reach. We were thus under great embarrassment, when a sentry, on the top of the hill, called out that he saw a boat crossing the river about three quarters of a mile above the house. I instantly directed Lieutenant Vincent with the soldiers of the 19th to seize it at all risks. On reaching the spot where the boat had been seen, he found it had been conveyed to the opposite side.

This obstacle was no sooner known than two gallant fellows, whose names it would be unfair to omit (Simon Gleason and Daniel Quin) volunteered to swim over and bring it back; which they boldly accomplished under protection of the fire of the party. Lieutenant Vincent instantly leaped into the boat with as many men as it would carry (between fifteen and twenty), and having crossed the river, marched quickly down its bank to take the enemy in flank. Panic-struck, the Candians deserted the battery, and fled in confusion at his approach. Such was the promptitude and decision with which this service was executed, that the whole was accomplished with only the loss of two men wounded. The Candians, formidable in their fastnesses, are so feeble in close combat, that in a quarter of an hour nearly the whole of that mass which had a short time before covered the opposite banks, and threatened our annihilation, had disappeared in the woods.

I lost no time in prosecuting our march; about two hundred yards in rear of the battery stands the palace of Condasaly, the king's favourite residence, a beautiful building, richly ornamented with the presents received by the kings of Candy from the Portuguese, Dutch, and English. This palace had been carefully preserved by General Macdowal in 1803. And the King had availed himself of this respect shown to it at that time to make it a principal *depôt* of arms and ammunition; which, as I was unable to remove, and it being my object to destroy, wherever found, I was under the necessity of setting the building on fire. We afterwards continued our march to the capital, expecting, from the firing heard in the morning, a speedy meeting with our countrymen forming the co-operating columns. Indeed, so confident was I of joining some of them, that I had the reports of my detachment made out ready to present to the officer commanding in the town.

Candasaly is only five miles from Candy, and the road good. When half way from hence to this capital, we passed a heavy Dutch gun which the enemy were bringing up to the battery on the river.

Our advanced guard had scarcely got within range of a temple which is situated on a hill above the town of Candy, when they sustained a volley of musketry; a few minutes afterwards I could plainly perceive the enemy flying through the streets in great confusion. It was now evident that none of the other divisions had arrived. After detaching Lieutenant Rogers with a party of *sepoys* to occupy the heights commanding the town, our troops once more took possession of the capital, which they found, as usual, entirely deserted by its inhabitants. The palace being in the most favourable situation for resisting any immediate attack, I took possession of it, and looked with great anxiety for the arrival of the other detachments.

7.—This day passed without any intelligence of our friends. Towards evening, a Malay officer and some soldiers formerly in our service, but forced into that of the Candians after Major Davie's surrender, arrived amongst us, and informed me, that a fortnight before a rumour had prevailed of six English divisions having entered the Candian territory; that many of his countrymen had accompanied the Candians to oppose these divisions, but had returned without having seen an enemy. It was generally believed that these divisions had been driven back.

He added that the Candians were in great force in the neighbour-hood, and delayed their attack only until the climate should begin to take effect upon us; and that the firing which Lieutenant Povelary had taken for that of our columns on the morning of the 6th was a re-joicing at our embarrassed situation, which seemed to them to admit neither of advance nor retreat, but to lead inevitably to surrender, and consequent massacre.

I was greatly at a loss what to make of this statement. The officer's character I knew to be respectable; and their report of the number of divisions corresponded exactly with the fact.

8.—Early this morning detached Lieutenant Povelary with a party to the top of the hills, to ascertain whether a camp, or any part of our troops, could be discerned. He brought no tidings of them.

In the forenoon, some gun *lascars*, who had been taken prisoners with Major Davie, effected their escape to us, and related that they had just returned from the frontiers, whither they had marched with a body of Candians for the purpose of opposing the English troops that were advancing into the country; that they had actually seen one detachment with whom their party had exchanged a few shots, by which a Candian chief was wounded; that soon after, this detachment marched back to the English territory, whereupon the whole corps in which they served was recalled to the capital; that a rumour prevailed amongst the Candians that all the English troops except my detach-ment were repulsed; that the king had proclaimed to his people that he had driven five English armies back to the sea, and that it only remained for them to chastise a few *banditti* who had stolen up from Batticolo.

My anxiety for the safety of my detachment had been hourly in-creasing since my arrival in Candy, and was now wrought up to the highest pitch. I considered its situation as eminently perilous. The army under General Macdowal had been only twenty days getting to Candy in 1803, though encumbered by six-pounders, and obliged to halt several days for want of *coolies*. The detachment that I conceived to be coming up were lighter, and consequently would have been enabled to march much quicker.

The distance from Columbo to Candy is only 103 miles, and that from Trincomalé, 142, and the roads from both places perfectly known whereas my route lay partly through the province of Ouva, the most mountainous and least known of the whole island; and, in consequence of my being obliged to make a circuit for the purpose of forming a junction with Colonel Maddison, amounted to 194 miles.

The time elapsed even since one of the detachments had been seen on the frontiers was enough, and more than enough, for its arrival; that they were driven back by the Candians, could not for a moment be believed. I considered the king's proclamation merely as an artifice to encourage his troops, yet the non-arrival of our divisions still continued to increase my surprise and uneasiness. Our provisions were now considerably reduced, and much of our ammunition expended. Our situation began also to make a powerful impression on the Europeans, as well as on the native troops.

The former, with the exception of a few artillerymen, consisted of the 19th regiment, a great part of which corps had been sacrificed the year before, under Major Davie. Many of these men had been in Candy with General Macdowal; the massacre was still fresh in their recollection. They saw displayed in savage triumph in several of the apartments of the palace, the hats, shoes, canteens, and accoutrements of their murdered comrades, most of them still marked with the names of their ill-fated owners.

I could easily collect, from the conversation of the officers, that few of them agreed with regard to what ought to be done. I therefore avoided calling a council of war, persuaded that it would only give rise to unpleasant differences. Added to this, the rains had already set in with considerable violence, and I was perfectly aware of the difficulty of passing the Candian River during the monsoon. Under these circumstances, to have remained longer in the capital would, in the event of the other divisions not arriving (of whose appearance there was now scarcely any hope), have occasioned the certain destruction of my detachment. On the other hand, should they come up (and I had no reason to doubt that one of them had been seen on the frontiers), what must the general think on finding that my detachment had thus returned without co-operation? Added to this, I had to dread the censure and disgrace that might result from a step thus precipitately taken.

Balancing between these opposite motives, the state of my mind, on this distressing occasion, it is impossible to describe; it can only be conceived by those who have had the misfortune to be placed in circumstances of similar anxiety.

Obliged to assume an air of gaiety amongst the troops, whilst my mind was agitated by the most melancholy reflections; feeling that not only the honour, but the life, of every man in the detachment depended on my conduct, I may truly say that even those individuals who were suffering around me from sickness and from wounds had no reason to envy the situation of their commander.

Though strongly prompted by my own feelings to continue following up what I deemed to be the object of my orders, I at this period regarded the safety of the detachment entrusted to my command as paramount to every other consideration. I therefore determined, in the first instance to cross the Candian River, so as, at all events, to ensure my retreat, and take post on the left bank, where I might wait a day or two longer for the tidings of the other detachments. I clearly foresaw that this movement would draw the whole of the enemy upon me, and consequently lead to a considerable expenditure of ammunition. They were in great force in the neighbourhood, and had for the last two days abstained from molesting us, waiting to see what steps I should pursue: yet of the two evils this appeared the least.

By encamping on the left bank of the river, we should be in readiness to co-operate with any of the other detachments that might arrive. We should also be enabled to retreat either on Columbo or Trincomalé, whereas returning by the Batticolo road was completely out of the question. In addition to its length, and the difficulties which the country presented, I knew that the Candians had been employed in blocking up the passes to prevent our return. Besides, I must have crossed the Mahavilla Gonga twice, at the fords of Padrepelly and Pangaram.

Having weighed these circumstances, I came to the resolution of marching out of Candy the next morning.

9.—At six a.m. commenced my march, abstaining from destroying or even injuring the town of Candy, that in the event of our troops still coming up, the followers might not be deprived of shelter. On the outside of the town, we passed a number of skeletons hanging on the trees, the remains of our massacred officers. We next reached the banks of the river, the scene of the cruel catastrophe which closed the career of Major Davie's detachment, and found the ground still covered with the bones of the victims. The river not being fordable, we were under the necessity of encamping on this ominous spot, while a party returned to Candy for materials to make rafts. Meanwhile the enemy were seen assembling in vast numbers on the opposite bank.

They took care to remind us of the danger of our situation, calling to us to observe the bones of our countrymen, and assuring us that ere long we should experience a similar fate. They repeatedly urged the natives to desert, as the only means of preserving their lives. It is but justice here to remark, that of the native troops, whether *sepoys* or Malays, not a man proved unfaithful to his colours. Even from the followers, I had hitherto experienced a degree of fidelity scarcely to be expected from their general character, not a man having yet deserted me. But our situation was now about to become too trying for their resolution.

At three p.m. two rafts were completed; but the current was so rapid that our tow-ropes immediately gave way. Punting was therefore the only expedient, and this was attended with much delay.

Late in the evening Lieutenant Rogers having crossed with a few Europeans, attacked and drove from the hill above the ferry a strong party of the enemy, with the loss of one of their chiefs who was bayoneted. This considerably checked their ardour. The greater part of the night was taken up in getting over our invalids.

10.—In the course of the morning, the river having fallen, some of the troops and followers forded it. We were also enabled to get over part of the stores. But towards noon the rain set in, and, as is usual in mountainous countries, the river became almost immediately too deep to be passed in that manner. By the rapidity of the current, one of our two small rafts was completely carried away, and the other became nearly unmanageable. Our tents, the 3rd company of *sepoys*, and our rear guard were still on the right bank of the river.

Apprehending that if these men were not quickly brought over, they would be lost to us for ever, I ordered them to cross without delay, which was effected with great difficulty by four o'clock, leaving the tents behind.

The constant skirmishing of the last two days had reduced our stock of ammunition to two small barrels of 800 rounds each, and several of the troops were without cartridges. Nearly two days had now elapsed since my departure from Candy; and no intelligence had reached me of the other detachments. I felt, therefore, the necessity of coming to an immediate decision relative to my future proceedings; and the troops and followers having now all passed, I determined without loss of time to commence my retreat.

The Trincomalé road, though longer, appeared upon the whole to present fewer obstacles than that leading to Columbo. In following the latter, we should have been under the necessity of taking by storm the two posts of Geeriagamme and Garlgaddray, situated at the top of the Columbo passes, through both of which the road runs. I therefore gave the preference to the former route. We were 142 miles from Trincomalé, with a road before us less rugged indeed in its nature than that which we had traversed, but in which we were likely to be equally exposed to annoyance from the enemy. As the bullocks would only impede our progress, I determined to leave them behind, and directing each soldier to take six days' rice on his back, abandoned the rest of the stores.

Whilst destroying the other stores, a parcel of loose powder, which had unfortunately been left near one of the boxes containing shells, took fire, which was immediately communicated to the fuses, and the shells continued to burst amongst us for some time, killing and wounding several of the *coolies* who were to have carried them, and desperately wounding a sergeant of artillery. This accident occasioned some confusion, of which the enemy took advantage, and commenced a general attack, with a trifling loss on our side; in which, however, they were repulsed.

About five o'clock in the afternoon, we were enabled to commence our march, our *coolies* carrying a long train of sick and wounded.

It was late before we reached the top of the Trincomalé pass, and the rain, the darkness, and the ruggedness of the mountains put it quite out of our power to descend. We here passed a distressing night, exposed to incessant rain, without the means of preparing victuals, and hearing the fall of the trees which the Candians were felling lower down on the mountain to obstruct our next day's march.

11.—Found the Candians posted on the different hills that command the pass, while the road was blocked up in many places with large trees, and in some with breastworks. After several hours' labour and exposure to the enemy's fire, we gained the bottom of the pass with the loss of five Europeans, eight *sepoys*, and thirty followers, killed and wounded; a loss considerable in itself, but smaller than I had expected from the opposition that awaited us. Here I was deprived of the services of Lieutenant Vincent, who received a wound in the thigh; a deprivation which I felt severely, from the very able assistance he had hitherto afforded me.

We now continued our route, proceeding very slowly on account of the great increase of our wounded. Towards evening we passed the ruins of Fort Macdowal, which the Candians had entirely destroyed, and halted only when the darkness and rain prevented us from finding our way further.

12.—Continued our march without stopping, harassed as usual by the enemy, who were indefatigable in blocking up the roads before us. During this morning, Lieutenant Smith, of the 19th, a most promising young officer, received a severe wound in the breast, which completely deprived me of his services. At five p.m. perceiving that the enemy had strongly fortified a hill over which we had to pass, I attacked and carried it by the bayonet, with the loss of two Europeans and five *sepoys* killed. On reaching the summit, we found the road so completely closed up, that we could not attempt to pursue it that night; and to aggravate our misfortune, we had lost the guides acquainted with this part of the country, two of them having deserted and one having been shot this day.

13.—As soon as it was daylight, I perceived a path lying in a northerly direction, which I followed as our only guide; concluding that if it did not conduct us to Trincomalé, it would lead to some of our other settlements.

The enemy this morning appeared more resolute than they had hitherto showed themselves. Led on by our own Malays and gun *lascars* who had formerly deserted to them, they attacked our line both in front and rear, and actually cut in amongst the *coolies*, who became perfectly panic-struck, threw down the sick and wounded, and either ran into the forests to conceal themselves, or rushed in among the troops, whom they threw into confusion. Unfortunately, two wounded Europeans, a sergeant of the Royal Artillery and a private of the 19th, who were in charge of the rear-guard, on this occasion fell into the hands of the enemy.

The Bengal *lascars* and Malays in the Candian service repeatedly addressed their countrymen in our ranks, informing them that the King of Candy did not consider them as his enemies, and promising that such of them as would come over to join him should be appointed captains in his army; but that, if they persisted in continuing with the Europeans, whom they represented as an impure beef-eating race, they would be massacred along with them, the moment they should fall into their hands. All these endeavours to shake the fidelity of the native troops, however, still continued unavailing. As the day advanced, the path became so narrow and intricate that I foresaw it would be impossible to make much farther progress after dark, without entangling the detachment in the woods. I therefore halted, and directed Lieutenant Virgo to go forward and order back the advanced guard with the sick and wounded.

This officer not returning, I sent on a corporal to know the cause of the delay, and to bring back a part of the 19th for the purpose of assisting to charge the enemy, who had by this time collected a considerable force in a village in our rear. The corporal returned, unable to find our advanced guard. I sent him forward again in quest of them with an escort, and after a considerable time had elapsed, he returned a second time, reporting that he had been three miles in front, without being able to gain the least intelligence of them, or even to trace what path they had followed. The enemy were now assembled in considerable force in our rear, with the apparent intention of closing with us. I determined immediately to charge them with the few Europeans belonging to the rear-guard and the native troops; leaving a strong party on the spot where we had been stationed, for the purpose of directing our vanguard (if they should return) to a village at some distance, where I intended to pass the night.

Our brave fellows advanced to the charge, gallantly led on by Lieutenants Povelary and Smith of the Bengal *sepoys*; they soon routed the Candians, and the few who still had strength to pursue, occasioned a considerable loss to the enemy. Among their slain, I was happy to find two of our Malay deserters, who had made themselves particularly conspicuous for the last three days, not only in animating the enemy, but in encouraging our men to desert. On this occasion, we took four large *gengals* and a quantity of muskets. The village afforded us shelter from the inclemency of the weather, and, what was still more welcome, a quantity of boiled rice.

Since our departure from Candy on the 9th, our only food had consisted of raw rice, which latterly had become musty and mildewed. We had been engaged in one continued skirmish, exposed without intermission alternately to a scorching sun and a violent rain; and glad at night, when we could get a stone or log of wood, to raise our heads from the wet ground. From seven o'clock till two, it generally continued fair, and the effects of the sun were powerfully felt. After two, the rain set in, and continued incessantly during the whole of the night.

14.—I was much concerned at the advanced guard not return-ing, and on resuming my march, followed the road which I thought it most likely they had taken. We had now the satisfaction to find that the enemy's pursuit had considerably slackened, owing chiefly to the spirited attack of the preceding evening, which showed them that, although weakened, we were far from being conquered; and owing in some measure also to the inconvenience they too suffered from the incessant rains. Passed this night in the woods without shelter.

15.—The enemy's fire continued to decrease; a few shots only were fired at us in the course of the day, and those without effect. Halted at night in a small village, where we were enabled to procure shelter, and some refreshment.

16.—Saw a few of the enemy at a distance; they did not attempt to molest us. We here found ourselves in the Trincomalé road. Halted at night in a small village a few miles from Minery Lake, where I was surprised to find the advanced guard with Lieutenant Virgo, but (pain-ful to add) without Lieutenants Vincent and Smith, and two wounded soldiers of the 19th. I was informed that Lieutenant Smith had died of his wounds; and there was every reason to suppose that Lieutenant Vincent had met a similar fate, or perhaps the more distressing one of falling into the merciless hands of the Candians.

Thus were lost to the service two excellent officers, in the prime of life, who had conducted themselves throughout this arduous ex-pedition with a degree of zeal, intrepidity, and perseverance, highly creditable to themselves, and consolatory to their friends. I shall ever regret the loss of these meritorious young men, from whose conduct I had on so many occasions derived considerable aid. The guard alleged that they had lost their way in the woods, and were nearly starved; that the *coolies* had completely deserted them; that they were themselves so exhausted as to be scarcely able to walk, and had no means of carry-ing the sick, whom they were under the necessity of abandoning; that they were without guides, and found their way to the village where we then were by mere chance. Considering Lieutenant Virgo as the cause, in the first instance, of this disaster, by not bringing back the guard, I ordered him into arrest.

This officer pleaded, in vindication of his conduct, that the soldiers had refused to obey his orders. On further inquiry, I found that the situation in which the soldiers were placed had in some degree shaken their discipline, and that they were even encouraged in insubordination by one of the non-commissioned officers, over whom Lieutenant Virgo, from belonging to another corps, had not sufficient control.

Under these circumstances, I thought it best to release this officer from arrest, and to submit the whole affair to the Commanding Officer of Trincomalé.

17.—Continued our march unmolested by the enemy, and passed the night in the woods.

18.—Reached the lake of Candelly, where we were again exposed to the inclemencies of the monsoon without the least shelter.

In proportion as the annoyance of the enemy slackened, and the necessity of personal exertion diminished, I had more time for reflection; and I may truly say, that the last few days of our march were not to me those in which I least suffered either in body or mind.

In common with the rest of the detachment, I had performed the greater part of the retreat barefooted. Had I possessed, indeed, changes of boots and shoes, I could not have used them, my feet having swelled, and become so tender from constant wet, that I could not without considerable pain put them to the ground.

In this condition, emaciated by fatigue, and labouring besides under a severe dysentery, arising, I presume, from the nature of the water, cold, and want of proper food, I was for the two last days obliged to be carried in my cloak, fastened to a stick.

These bodily sufferings, however, severe as they were, were only shared in common with many of those around me, and fell far short of the anguish of my mind. Whilst I witnessed the melancholy state of my brave companions, I could not help reflecting, that, perhaps, my precipitate retreat from Candy had brought all this distress and misery upon them; that the other divisions were possibly now in Candy, carrying into execution the general's plans; and that, in such case, I must, by my premature retreat, incur the censure of the general, and perhaps of the whole army.

On the other hand, in the event of our troops not coming up, I was satisfied that, had I remained a single day longer in Candy, the river, from the constant rains which we had experienced, would have become completely impassable; that our provisions would have been expended, without the possibility of procuring any fresh supply; and that, though determined not to capitulate under any extremity, we must, in the end, have been over-powered, owing to the want of ammunition, as well as from the pressure of sickness and famine.

While my mind was agitated by these conflicting reflections, we arrived at Tamblegamme on the 19th, where we were met by some officers from Trincomalé, who had heard that morning of our approach.

No words can express my surprise on now learning, for the first time, that it was not intended that I should proceed to Candy; that the general, on arriving at Jaffnapatam, had found obstacles to the combined attack, which he considered to be insurmountable—(the principal of these I have since understood to be the want of *coolies*; but of this, or of any other impediment to the success of the expedition, I was at the time totally unapprised)—that the orders of the 8th were intended as a countermand of the former plan; and that my having gone to Candy was deemed a disobedience of orders; that it was merely meant that the divisions should enter those parts of the enemy's territory adjacent to their respective districts, and return after laying waste the country; that the other five divisions had accordingly made these incursions, and had long since returned; and that the government, having learnt from the Cingalese on the borders of my detachment having been in Candy, had despaired of our ever returning.

It does not become me to decide on the origin of this unfortunate mistake, or to pronounce whether the fault lay in the orders, or in my interpretation of them.

The general, on making the tour of our stations, had taken great pains to explain to me the nature of his plans, the ultimate object of which was the possession of Candy; nor did he, in the various conversations I had the honour to hold with him on that subject, seem to entertain any doubt of the practicability of the proposed plan of operations.

These conversations were followed by an order to march, transmitted from Trincomalé; and so fully convinced was I that everything was in a complete state of preparation, that I considered the orders of the 8th in no other light than as a modification of the preceding instructions, as a change of the day of march and of the route; I never entertained the most distant idea that *the plan* was relinquished; as, after the devastation of that part of the country pointed out in the instructions, no ulterior object being presented, the original purport of the occupation of the enemy's capital remained unrevoked, and consequently to be followed up.

Cut off as I was by the remoteness of Batticolo from any intercourse with the other stations, I had no intimation of the changes that had taken place with respect to the destination of the other columns, to the commanders of which the orders had, it seems, been more explicit.

I hope that it may be allowed me to remark, that the general had seen some of them more recently than he had communicated with me; that the territory adjoining their districts was in general better known, and of course susceptible of clearer description than the province of Ouva. It appeared, however, necessary that an affair attended with such serious consequences should undergo investigation, and I was ordered round to Columbo, where a Court of Inquiry was held upon my conduct. The decision of the court was, that I had not disobeyed my orders in going to Candy.

The success of so small a force in penetrating unsupported to the Candian capital, and afterwards effecting its retreat, created considerable surprise throughout the island. The capital had never before been attempted with so inconsiderable a force. The troops under General Macdowal, in 1803, exceeded 3,000 men, and those the flower of the Ceylon Army. I have before remarked, that 1,000 men were even considered necessary to defend the town during the monsoon, though protected by works; and intervening events had rendered the Candians more formidable. They had gained to their service 500 well-disciplined Malays and *sepoys*, with a number of gun *lascars*, and 1,000 stand of serviceable English muskets, with a supply of ammunition. The continued skirmishes in which they had been engaged with us since that period, together with their occasional successes, had made them more expert, and given them a greater degree of confidence than they had at the commencement of the war.

A larger force than had been employed under General Macdowal and Lieutenant-Colonel Barbut was, therefore, prepared for the combined attack. Of the six divisions, mine was not only the smallest in point of numbers, but certainly the worst equipped.

Colonel Maddison, who commanded the Hambingtotte detachment, with which I was to have formed a junction at the entrance of the province of Ouva, I now learnt did not receive my letter till after his return, and his guides led him into a part of the country where there was no water to be procured; consequently he was under the necessity of changing his route; and instead of advancing to the northward and westward and entering Ouva, where his presence, though we might not have met, would have embarrassed the enemy, he was forced to keep entirely to the southward, so that I derived no assistance from the co-operation of that officer.

The other four divisions which entered the enemy's country, had they remained long enough, would have caused a powerful diversion in my favour; but, after having carried into execution their instructions, the completion of which required but a few days, they returned to their respective districts, where the whole of them had arrived some days before I reached the capital. It was on the return of these detachments that the king issued the proclamation, stating that he had driven five English armies back to the sea.

Thus the Candians were enabled to bring their whole force, which had been completely put in motion for the purpose of opposing all our divisions, against my detachment alone; with which, too, the king had every cause to be exasperated, in consequence of our having burnt his favourite palace of Condasaly, as well as that near Pangaram.

Harassed continually by the enemy, with, latterly, not a round of ammunition to return his fire (the few cartridges which were preserved by some of the Europeans as their last hope, being rendered useless by the rain, and their muskets entirely unserviceable), it cannot be surprising that our loss should have been great. In these respects the enemy had the advantage of us, their powder being preserved from damp in cocoa-nut shells, and their arms provided with guards made of skin or waxed cloth, which completely secured the locks from wet. But the Candians were not our only enemies, we had to contend with hunger, fatigue, extremes of heat and cold, besides all the diseases incidental to so unhealthy a climate.[2]

At an early stage of the retreat, I had been obliged to leave behind me the *doolies*, from the impossibility of getting them on, in consequence of abattis and other obstacles being placed in the line of our march. Many of the *coolies* had been either killed or wounded, several had deserted, and of those that remained few were in a situation to carry a burthen.

I was, therefore, obliged to have the men whose cases were the most

---

2. The following instances are convincing proofs of the insalubrity of the interior of Ceylon. On the 13th of March, 1803, the grenadier company of the 65th, under Captain Bullock, consisting of 3 officers and 75 men, marched from Columbo for Cattadinia, a small post in the interior. At the end of the month, without any loss by the enemy, the whole fell victims to the climate, excepting Lieutenant Hutchins and two privates. They were all robust young men, from 18 to 23 years of age, and had only landed from the Cape of Good Hope early in November. On the 11th of April, 400 men of the 51st regiment appeared under arms at Columbo, on their arrival from Candy. In little more than two months 300 of them were buried, having laid the foundation of disease in the interior.

desperate, carried along on cloths fastened to poles, whilst the others got on by leaning on their less exhausted comrades. Our progress was consequently very slow; nor was it, for the first three days, permitted us to halt, during the day, even for a single moment, to dress our wounded men, the least delay enabling the enemy to oppose fresh obstacles to our retreat. Latterly, when less pressed by the enemy, it was out of the surgeon's power to be of much assistance to the wounded, the *coolie* who carried the medicines and instruments having deserted; consequently the wounds in general became ill-conditioned, and at length so offensive to the patients themselves as scarcely to be borne.

Those of the detachment who had hitherto escaped sickness and wounds, were emaciated, sallow, and debilitated to an extreme degree. They were almost all barefooted; and many of those who had escaped the fire of the enemy, fell victims, after our arrival at Trincomalé, to the effects of their previous sufferings. Amongst those, I am sorry to mention Lieutenant Rogers, of the Bengal *sepoys*, who died of a fever a few days after his return. This officer, by his exertions during the retreat, and especially after I had lost the services of Lieutenants Vincent and Smith, had, by his activity and zeal, rendered most essential services to the detachment. He was ever foremost in danger.

To the exertions, indeed, and animating example of the officers in general, and the persevering courage of the soldiers, particularly those of the Royal Artillery and 19th, may be principally attributed the safety of the detachment.

RETURN OF KILLED, WOUNDED, AND MISSING OF THE DETACHMENT UNDER THE COMMAND OF CAPTAIN JOHNSTON.

Detail.	Royal Artill.		19th Regiment.					Malay Regiment.						Bengal Sepoys.					
	Sergeants.	Bombardiers.	Subldars.	Serjeants.	Corporals.	Drummers.	Privates.	European Lieutenant.	Malay Captain.	Malay Lieutenant.	Serjeants.	Corporals.	Privates.	Lieutenants.	Jemadars.	Havildars.	Naigues.	Drummers.	Privates.
Killed		1			1		4						3			1	1	1	9
Wounded	1			1	2		2						4			1	1		27
Missing			2				2									1			12
Total	1	1	2	1	3		8						7			3	2	1	48

N.B.—Owing to the great desertion (during the latter part of the march) amongst the *coolies* and pioneers, the amount of their killed and wounded could never be ascertained; but there is every reason to believe it was very considerable.

Having now related the whole of the circumstances which attended the detachment I had the honour to command during its march to Candy and in its retreat, I must still trespass on the attention of my readers to make a few observations connected with the subject.

With respect to the policy or expediency of invading the Candian territory, occupying the capital, cutting roads through the country, or dividing it into several governments, these are considerations, which, however important in their nature, do not come within the scope of my design. The propriety of such measures must greatly depend upon existing circumstances, of which the government for the time being must be supposed to be the best qualified to judge. This much, however, I think I may venture to suggest, from some experience of the Candian character; that, considering that each European soldier, at his arrival in India, costs the nation at least £100, these objects, even in a financial view of the subject, might be much better attained by the application of a smaller sum to secure, if necessary, an influence at the Court of Candy.

But should it be deemed more expedient to have recourse to arms as the best mode of maintaining and extending our ascendancy in Ceylon, I am not without hope that my remarks will be of service to those who may in future be appointed to conduct our military expeditions into the interior of that country. They are perhaps the more necessary, as of the few survivors of the last war, whose experience might be useful, scarcely any are now remaining in the island.

What I shall first advert to, as being of most essential importance to our military operations, not only in Ceylon, but in every part of India, is the expediency of European officers learning the native languages.

The disadvantages arising from an ignorance of the language of a people whom we command, or with whom we have to negotiate, have been so frequently exemplified in Ceylon, without an adequate remedy having been applied to the evil, that I think it necessary here to offer my sentiments on the subject.

The circumstance of being obliged to carry on a conversation by means of an interpreter, forms an almost insuperable bar to confidential intercourse, or acquiring secret information. Many of the Candians are well disposed to communicate the information they possess, in the expectation of reward; but in common with the natives of every part of India, are unwilling to commit themselves in the presence of an interpreter, in whose secrecy they cannot confide, knowing that if betrayed, not only their own lives, but the lives of their families will be forfeited, and their property confiscated.

The troops are also in a great measure placed in the power of the interpreter. Through the medium of the questions which he is instructed to put to the guides and spies, he is enabled to penetrate into the views of the commanding officer, and to betray them to the enemy; or, in stating their answers, he may deceive him, by altering, or entirely withholding, information of the greatest importance. The interpreter is ready enough to perceive, and to avail himself of the advantages of his situation. He takes care to place his own particular friends about the commanding officer's person. He holds a sort of court at the place of private residence, to which the guides and spies, or others who have business with the commanding officer, resort, in order to prepare their statements.

Thus the spies, who ought never to know each other, get acquainted; and the advantages which might be derived from comparing their different accounts, are, from their opportunities of communication with each other, totally lost. The interpreter, being the immediate executive agent, at once gains an ascendancy over all the natives in the camp, which he not unfrequently abuses; and however ill he may treat them, they never presume to complain, it being a maxim with the natives of India never to complain of a man in power. In this case, also, they are deterred by the consideration, that the person complained against forms their only channel of communication with the commanding officer.

When the natives know that the commanding officer understands their language, and that he does not make a confidant of the interpreter, who is generally the *Modiliar*,[3] they are ever ready to come forward with their information.

Of the great caution observed by the natives of India in respect to what they declare in public, or before interpreters, I have known some striking instances, wherein men have given testimonies, even upon

---

3. In Ceylon the native chiefs of districts, and many subordinate officers, have been designated *Modiliars*; which title, at an early period of the Portuguese government of the island, seems to have been peculiar to the chiefs of the *military* class; although now held by those who exercise not only the command of *Lascoryns* (the ancient soldiers of the country), but various civil functions in the districts of Ceylon.

oath, directly opposite to what they had previously stated to me in private and confidential communication; and upon being afterwards reproached for the contradiction, they have persisted in asserting that their *private statement* was the *true* one, the declarations which they had made on oath being prompted by fear of giving evidence in a public court, which would tend to injure the cause of one of the chiefs who had great power and influence in the country; that as it was uncertain how long I might remain in command of the district, the offended chief would, sooner or later, find the means of ruining the party; and that the consequences would not even stop here, but the children of the chief would continue to his children the hereditary vengeance of their father.

A knowledge of the language also enables us to converse with the men of education among the natives, who are generally communicative and well informed, particularly with what relates to their own country—a species of knowledge of which we stand the most in need. It farther enables us to peruse the writings, and, by instructing us in their origin, teaches us to respect prejudices of which the Indians are extremely tenacious, and which we are too apt at first landing to despise. What great political advantages might be derived from a proper management of these prejudices, experience has amply shown.

In a contempt of them, and in an ignorance of the country languages, have originated many of the greatest misfortunes which have befallen us in India. All officers who have served long in that country, whether in the King's or Company's service, must have had personal experience of the great advantages that are to be derived, both in respect to politics and military operations, from a knowledge of the languages: even the reputation of this knowledge will attract to an officer unreserved confidence in communication, and secure him from being deceived by false reports.

In the management of the native corps, ignorance of the language is attended with many and great disadvantages. The officer is in that case obliged to employ some native soldier as an interpreter; and those of this class who have, in menial situations, learned to speak a little English, are generally the most unworthy of confidence.

Men of this description, for the most part educated in the kitchens of Europeans, or servants in barracks or hospitals, acquire a degree of quickness and intelligence that renders them useful as orderlies, or in other capacities about the persons of European officers, who do not understand the country languages.

On courts-martial, or in matters of grievance or disputes which the soldiers may wish to submit to their officers, their statements come through these men: but as a trifling bribe will incline them to either side, the disadvantage of being obliged to have recourse to their assistance is obvious.

The species of influence which they acquire among the soldiers, from their situation, is almost always abused by them. They even assume more authority than the oldest native commissioned or non-commissioned officers, who may be men of caste and education, whose orders they not only frequently presume to dispute, but encourage others to do the same. This assumption of authority is for the most part acquiesced in, from the danger of complaining against a man who so frequently has it in his power to injure by misrepresenting the complainant to his officers, whose ignorance of the language leaves him at the mercy of his interpreter.

Having pointed out the evil, I shall now endeavour to suggest the remedy. The officers belonging to the regular regiments of the line stationed in Ceylon, who are not permanently attached to the island, have no motive to exert themselves in applying to the languages of the country. In the native corps, however, we might expect to find this species of local knowledge. But the Ceylon regiments have been hitherto officered from the line, and many of the captains and field-officers nominated in England. They consequently, on their arrival, find themselves in the command of men whose language they do not understand, and who do not understand theirs.

All communications between them are, of course, carried on by means of interpreters. There being no inducements to a permanent residence in Ceylon, either in respect to society, allowances, or scope for military enterprise, it is the wish of every officer to leave it as soon as possible. Under the present state of the establishment, all the exertions of the officers of the native corps (who can never otherwise expect to be removed), are directed to procure an exchange into the line; and hence frequent changes take place in those regiments—a circumstance which totally prevents their applying to the native languages, a knowledge of which can be useful there only.

Whilst the service continues to labour under these disadvantages, the evil must remain in full force. It would, therefore, appear necessary that it should in some measure become local, like that of the East India Company's establishments; and that military promotion should be made in some measure dependent on a knowledge of the native languages. They would in that case consider themselves as permanently settled on the island, and look upon their regiments as their homes. Under such a plan, no officer could arrive at any important command without being thoroughly acquainted with the language and customs of the country. And the general would then find amongst his officers, in whose honour he could confide, every species of local knowledge of which he would stand in need; instead of being obliged to seek for it amongst *Modiliars*, interpreters, and native orderlies.

On the Dress of the Ceylon Troops.

I will now beg leave to submit a few observations on the dress of our troops in Ceylon, which, experience has shown, is ill adapted to the country and species of warfare in which they are likely to be employed.

In making these observation, the result of local experience, I trust I shall not be considered as interfering unbecomingly with the existing regulations of the army, the efficiency of which, so far as they relate to the dress and equipment of the troops acting in our distant colonies, may be best ascertained by those officers who have served with them; as one of whom (but with the utmost deference to the authority of men more competent to discuss and decide on the subject) I merely submit my opinion.

Situated as England now is with her colonies, so extensive in themselves, so widely dispersed, and consequently embracing a variety of climates, it seems obvious that we must be guided in a great degree in the formation and dress of our troops (particularly those raised in the colonies), by the climate and nature of the country in which they are to serve, and by the description of enemy against whom they are most likely to contend; as well as by the character, habits, and prejudices of the people who compose these corps.

Surely the same dress which is adapted to the snows of Canada would not answer in the burning plains of Hindostan; nor ought the same tactics that are practised in Europe, where armies are formed with numerous and well-appointed bodies of cavalry, and immense trains of artillery, be resorted to in the mountains of Ceylon, where a horse is scarcely known, and where the smallest piece of ordnance cannot be transported without the greatest difficulty.

The great objects to which we should direct our attention (next to the health of the soldier), are a celerity of movement, and a facility of approaching the enemy unperceived, so as to take him by surprise.

Throughout the late war the Candians always showed a disposition to avoid our troops in the open field, by immediately betaking themselves to the woods or mountains the instant they had notice of our approach, from whence they could keep up a galling fire on our line, or whatever division of our troops became, from their situation, most favourable for this mode of attack; and unless an opportunity presented itself of stealing on them unawares, we scarcely ever could boast of doing much execution.

In a country so mountainous and woody as the interior of Ceylon, where the route must frequently wind through narrow and rugged defiles, or over heights ascended with vast labour and fatigue, it is of great consequence that the soldier should be freed as much as possible from every unnecessary encumbrance, in order to lessen the comparative disadvantages under which he is to act against an enemy whose only covering is a cloth wrapped round his loins, in the fold of which is deposited a cocoa-nut shell containing his gunpowder, with a few dozen balls, and who is, moreover, familiar with every little path by which he may advance or retreat. It is easy to conceive how difficult it must be for our troops, toiling as they are accustomed to do under heavy burdens, ever to come up with such an enemy but by surprise.

The rays of the sun, however, reflected from the bright arms and large brass plates in front of the soldier's cap, together with his red jacket, white pantaloons, and white belts, discover him to the enemy from a considerable distance, and not only render any surprise by day impossible, but point him out as a fair object for the enemy's marksmen. Of the comparative disadvantages arising from our dress I had frequently the most striking proofs, in being able to discover any movement of our troops at the distance of several miles, merely by the glittering of their arms and appointments; whereas, though at the same time surrounded by thousands of the enemy, I could scarcely distinguish a man.

In order, therefore, to remedy these disadvantages, I would in the first instance suggest, that, for the common musket, be substituted one of a lighter kind (for instance, a carbine), and that the barrel be stained like that of our light regiments. I would also provide every lock with a guard composed of skin or oilcloth, which would always preserve it dry and efficient. The heavy dews, which constantly fall during the nights, have the same effect on the foliage of the woods as that produced by violent rain; thus it frequently happened, that, from the soldier's being incapable of securing his arms or the lock from the wet, when marching through a close country, his musket became utterly unserviceable; while the enemy, who invariably adopted the above plan, were generally enabled (even during a heavy rain) to keep up a constant fire from the midst of their woods, where it was impossible for us to penetrate, in order to dislodge them with the bayonet.

With respect to the colour of the uniform, it ought to assimilate as much as possible to that of the surrounding objects. I would, therefore, recommend a green or grey jacket and trowsers, black belts, with a hat free from all those ornaments now in use, which serve to draw on the soldier the fire of the enemy.

The present cap appears, indeed, but ill calculated for the Ceylon troops; as, in addition to the warmth that a large heated brass plate must naturally communicate to the head, all the lower part of the soldier's head and neck is entirely exposed to the sun and rain; and there being nothing to convey the water that falls on the cap over the cape of his jacket, it consequently runs down his back, and he finds himself wet to the skin long before it has penetrated his great coat. Thus circumstanced, he becomes cold and chilly, if not in continual motion; and when on duty at night, or without the means of procuring dry clothes, it must lay the foundation of many diseases, but particularly that known by the name of the jungle fever, which generally proved so fatal to our troops when serving in the interior.

The glazed peak in front of the cap reflects the glare from the hot sand on the eyes, which for the time is unpleasant, and must in the end injure the sight.

Some regiments adopted an entire glazed leather cap, which is assuredly much worse than the beaver, as it becomes in a short time infinitely more heated, and as soon as the soldier begins to perspire, the leather becomes moist, and attaches itself so closely to the head as to prevent all circulation of fresh air within; the confined air then, from the heat occasioned by the warm leather as well as that of the man's head, soon becomes many degrees warmer than the atmosphere.

These caps were introduced in Ceylon a short time before I left it; and I always found that the sentries and soldiers, who were for any time exposed to the sun, complained of headaches, which they attributed to the cap. I can speak from my own experience, that even at a common field-day, though in the morning, before the sun became very powerful, I was regularly attacked by a violent headache, which generally continued during the remainder of the day; though, after a much longer exposure to the sun, even during the heat of the day

61

(when in a round hat), I felt little inconvenience.

Another disadvantage attending these caps is, that from the great trouble of cleaning them, the soldiers were in the habit, when out of sight of the officers, to take them from their heads, and carry them in a cloth, to prevent the varnish from being melted by the sun or injured by the rain; thus rather choosing to expose their bare heads to the weather than undergo the labour of repolishing them.

White, from its being the greatest non-conductor of heat, is therefore best calculated for warm climates.

The following extract from Dr. Franklin, on the subject of heat, may not perhaps prove uninteresting or useless:—

As to the different degrees of heat imbibed from the sun's rays by cloths of different colours, since I cannot find the notes of my experiment to send you, I must give it as well as I can from memory.

But first let me mention an experiment you may easily make yourself. Walk but a quarter of an hour in your garden when the sun shines, with a part of your dress white, and a part black; then apply your hand to them alternately, and you will find a very great difference in their warmth. The black will be quite hot to the touch, the white still cool.

Another. Try to fire the paper with a burning glass. If it is white, you will not easily burn it, but if you bring the focus to a black spot, or upon letters, written or printed, the paper will immediately be on fire under the letters.

Thus fullers and dyers find black cloths, of equal thickness with white ones, and hung out equally wet, dry in the sun much sooner than the white, being more readily heated by the sun's rays. It is the same before a fire; the heat of which sooner penetrates black stockings than white ones, and so is apt sooner to burn a man's shins. Also beer much sooner warms in a black mug set before the fire, than in a white one, or in a bright silver tankard.

My experiment was this. I took a number of little square pieces of broadcloth from a tailor's pattern-card, of various colours. There were black, deep blue, lighter blue, green, purple, red, yellow, white, and other colours, or shades of colours. I laid them all out upon the snow in a bright sunshiny morning. In a few hours (I cannot now be exact as to the time) the black, being warmed most by the sun, was sunk so low as to be below the stroke of the sun's rays; the dark blue almost as low, the lighter blue not quite so much as the dark, the other colours less as they were lighter; and the quite white remained on the surface of the snow, not having entered it at all.

What signifies philosophy that does not apply to some use? May we not learn from hence, that black clothes are not so fit to wear in a hot sunny climate or season as white ones; because in such clothes the body is more heated by the sun when we walk abroad, and are at the same time heated by the exercise, which double heat is apt to bring on putrid dangerous fevers? That soldiers and seamen, who must march and labour in the sun, should in the East or West Indies have an uniform of white? That summer hats, for men or women, should be white, as repelling that heat which gives headaches to many, and to some the fatal stroke that the French call the *coup de soleil?*

That the ladies' summer hats, however, should be lined with black, as not reverberating on their faces those rays which are reflected upwards from the earth or water? That the putting a white cap of paper or linen *within* the crown of a black hat, as some do, will not keep out the heat, though it would if placed *without?* That fruit-walls being blacked, may receive so much heat from the sun in the day-time, as to continue warm in some degree through the night, and thereby preserve the fruit from frosts, or forward its growth?—with sundry other particulars of less or greater importance, that will occur from time to time to attentive minds?

But it might be objected to in Ceylon, as producing the very evils I would endeavour to correct, that of rendering the soldier too conspicuous. I would recommend, then, a light brown hat, with a brim sufficiently broad to protect the lower part of the head and neck against the sun or rain, and also to conduct the water over the cape of the jacket, without being too large to interfere with the perfect use of the musket; the under part of the brim to be green, as a relief to the eyes.

It might also be advisable to have the hat a slight degree larger than the head, to allow of a pad between it and the forehead, for the purpose of leaving an open space round the temples to admit of a free circulation of air.

This kind of hat might appear to some unbecoming; but we must recollect, that the health and comfort of the soldier should be our first consideration.

Of the Carriage of Baggage and Stores.

There is nothing that embarrasses more the operations of our Ceylon forces than the carriage of baggage and stores.

The general mode of conveyance is either by bullocks or *coolies*. Elephants have been also used; but I do not think them well calculated for such a service on this island. Their movements are slow; they are soon fatigued; and, unless long accustomed to the sound, easily alarmed at the firing. They are a good mark for the enemy, and when wounded apt to become unmanageable; in which case the march may even be wholly stopped, as one of these animals, with his load, will completely fill up a narrow pass. When exasperated, the *coolies* are afraid to approach him. If his wounds are such as to prevent his proceeding, his load is generally obliged to be left behind; a loss that is much more felt than that of the loads of a few *coolies*.

In the choice between bullocks and *coolies*, when either can be had, we must be guided by the nature of the expedition upon which the troops are to be employed. If the detachment be large, and likely to remain long in the interior, bullocks are preferable, because their keep will not diminish the stores, whilst the *coolies* would soon eat up their own loads.

The bullocks are of two sorts. They are either the immediate property of government, or belonging to the inhabitants, and are furnished by the different villages upon requisition. In the latter case, it is always desirable that the proprietors should have charge of them, and be obliged to carry their bags and saddles along with them. The cattle will thus be taken care of, the loads properly balanced, and their backs preserved sound.

The bullocks which are the property of government are usually given in charge to *lascars*, or common *coolies*, who, having no particular interest in their preservation, are careless in putting on their loads, and neglect to put cloths under them. Thus in a few days the poor animals' backs are dreadfully galled; and, if the greatest care be not taken, their sores fester, and are filled with maggots: notwithstanding which, the drivers will continue to load them, with the greatest indifference. They will also, in order to save themselves the trouble of looking after their cattle, frequently fasten seven or eight of them to a log of wood, by way of security, which, by preventing them from grazing in a manner sufficient for their support, soon reduces them to a state wholly unfit for any kind of service.

In order to prevent these inconveniences, it would be advisable to put the bullocks in several small divisions, each under the care of a Congany or Tindal, who should be answerable for the treatment of the bullocks of his divisions; and experienced drivers, accustomed to the care of cattle and to load them properly, should be employed. It would be also desirable that some trustworthy non-commissioned officer should be directed to examine the backs of the cattle daily, and to see that their loads are properly adjusted.

If, on the other hand, the detachment be small, and only intended for an incursion for a few days into the enemy's country, when everything will depend upon rapidity of movement, bullocks will not be found to answer; their pace is much too slow for such operations, and it is almost impossible to get them on by night. *Coolies* alone will here answer the purpose; and with them a great deal of management is necessary. The common mode of making up their loads in gunny bags, used for holding rice on shipboard and in stores, is liable to two objections.

1st.—They afford no defence against the weather, the rain penetrating the bags, and mildewing the rice.

2ndly.—The cloth of which the bags are made is very coarse, and badly sewed; and the rice consequently makes its way through the interstices. The *coolies*, also, nothing reluctant to diminish their burdens, will often widen the seams. Thus the route of a detachment may frequently be traced for several miles by the grain strewed on the road.

This waste may in some measure be prevented by doubling the bags. But there is nothing equal to the common bags made of mats, which the natives use for their *pingoes*, or loads; they not only prevent waste, but keep the rice long dry.

The *coolies* frequently plunder their loads; an evil which it is not easy to remedy, as by slipping into the woods unperceived, the *coolie* can take out of his gunny bag as much rice as he chooses, and, having concealed it in his cloth, returns to his comrades without having been missed.

The best method of preventing this waste appears to be this. Let the quantity of rice sufficient to load all his people be served out to each Congany, for which he is to be held responsible; and let him be punished in case of any remarkable defalcation, making a proper allowance for inevitable wastage. He is the only man capable of checking their thefts. But it is necessary to keep a good look-out on the Congany himself, as it is a common practice among the Conganies to sell the rice entrusted to their care.

The same precautions are necessary with regard to the bullock drivers. Here, too, the bags used by the natives should be employed.

To persons not accustomed to the species of service which I have been describing, these observations may appear trivial. But they will think otherwise, when they consider that we are speaking of a country in which, if the stock of provisions with which a detachment or an army sets out is either wasted or expended prematurely, it is for the most part impossible to procure a fresh supply. A commanding officer, who should unwisely contemn these precautions, might find himself in the disgraceful and dangerous predicament of discovering, when he expected to have provisions enough left for twenty days, that his stock, having been reduced by plunder or neglect, could not last beyond half the period.

By these circumstances alone, after having incurred considerable expense towards an expedition, the whole enterprise might be frustrated, and the lives of many valuable soldiers sacrificed.

GUIDES.

The necessity of experienced guides, so great in all military operations, is more particularly urgent in a country like the interior of Ceylon, intricate in its own nature, and to the knowledge of which we have no access by the usual means of maps.

The difficulty of procuring good guides is very great. There are, it is true, always men ready to undertake for hire the task of conducting our troops through the Candian country; but these are either Candian emigrants, who have settled in our possessions, or *Lubbies*.[4] These persons are in general perfectly well acquainted with the common paths that lead from one village to another, and, in consequence, imagine themselves qualified to fulfil the office of guides. This might, no doubt, be the case, were our troops always to march in daylight, and by these

4. A sect of Mohammedans, supposed to be the descendants of Arab traders, who, at a remote period, mixed with the natives of India, and settled chiefly on the coasts of Malabar and Coromandel. They conduct the chief interior trade of Ceylon, and much of that with the neighbouring coasts. They are considered by the other Mohammedans as a degenerate race, and their character in India bears a near resemblance to that of the *Jews* in Europe.

paths only.

But as circumstances often require that parties should be sent in various directions about the country, and particularly at night, the most favourable time for attacking the enemy, in such cases, the Lubbies, as they only know the high-roads, can give little or no assistance; and it is seldom that natives, even of the spot on which the operations are to be conducted, are sufficiently acquainted with all the paths and turnings in the forests, to enable them to conduct troops through them at night. In these thick forests it is so dark that, even in the brightest moonlight, it is extremely difficult, and often impossible, for one not perfectly acquainted with the track to discern the footpath.

The indolence of the Cingalese seldom allowing of their clearing away any extent of ground, and the rapidity of vegetation, are other circumstances which increase the difficulty. It is the practice of the inhabitants of each village to join once a-year, for the purpose of cutting away the trees for a considerable extent. After they have remained for some time on the ground till they are dry, they set them on fire, and burn all the branches and light wood, leaving the stumps, which they never root up, as well as the trunks, untouched. This process in some measure clears the ground, which is then hoed, and sown with what is called dry grain. This ground is called by the natives *Chanass*. It is found that soil which has been manured by the leaves rotting upon it for thirty or forty, or, perhaps, a hundred years, and by the ashes of the burnt wood, yields an excellent crop.

It is seldom sown above one season, being allowed the year following to run to wood, and fresh spots successively cleared away. Thus, in the course of two or three years, the face of the country is much changed; and a guide, who expects to traverse miles of forest, finds himself all at once in a large *chanass*. Here the ground is interspersed with stumps, and strewed with trunks of trees, through which it is extremely difficult to march by night. The guide may generally discern the borders of the forest on the opposite side; but, the paths having been effaced by cultivation, he can seldom know at what part to enter. Afraid to confess his ignorance, he goes on entangling the party more and more in the forest, where they wander about all night, finding themselves in the morning, perhaps, many miles distant from the post which was to have been surprised.

Neither can any advantage be derived in such situations from a compass. It being impossible to march in a direct line through a thick forest, intersected in many places by rivers and swamps, it is by the paths alone that we must be directed. On such occasions, an officer sent to surprise a post cannot be supposed to find his way to it by working a traverse course.

It may also often happen that the guide is in the pay of the enemy, and may first entangle the troops in the forest, and then leave them. It is, therefore, always proper to have him fastened to one of the soldiers. But admitting that the man has no evil intention, it must be extremely difficult for him, from the circumstances stated, to conduct troops properly to the place of their destination.

Seeing, then, how much depends, particularly in night enterprises, on the experience and fidelity of the guides, it behoves us to spare neither pains in procuring proper persons, nor expense in rewarding those who faithfully discharge their duty.

Modiliars.

Having, in the former part of this work, given some striking instances of treachery on the part of the *Modiliars*, it is but justice to declare that it was not meant to convey a general censure on that body. On the contrary, I know there are now in Ceylon some men in that capacity who have served the Dutch and English Governments with fidelity, and enjoy the reputation of high honour; and I have myself derived the greatest assistance from the zeal and exertions of the Modiliar of Batticolo, not only whilst in command of that district, but during the whole of my march to and from Candy.

I would take the liberty to recommend as the best line of policy, that our officers, whilst, having the fate of Constantine De Sáa and his army in their recollection, they guard against reposing too blind a confidence in the *Modiliars*, should carefully conceal from them the doubts which may be entertained of their fidelity, and treat them on all occasions with respect; these people being extremely sensible to slights, and particularly in the presence of their countrymen.

Coolies.

I think it right here to call the attention of the officer to the situation of a class of men, essential to all our military operations in India, without whose aid, indeed, we cannot make the smallest movement. I mean the *coolies*. Besides the humanity due to them as fellow-creatures, policy requires that this class of men should be treated with attention and kindness. Hitherto I am sorry to say that they have met with too little consideration in all our military operations.

It will be proper, on the line of march, to allow time to the *coolies*, who are not provided with *Talipot* leaves, and even to encourage them to construct huts or *wigwams* with branches and leaves. By this means their healths might be in a great measure preserved, and, what is of no less importance, they would be more reconciled to the service.

It is also essential that the commander of the troops should superintend the payment of the *coolies* in person, or by an European officer; as, when the payment is left to their native chiefs, they are frequently defrauded, even to half the amount of their pay, and the odium thrown on the commanding officer.

In issuing or explaining orders either to the common *coolies*, or their chiefs, we cannot be too explicit. Many of the interpreters understand English but imperfectly; and when they do not comprehend the order, rather than confess their ignorance by asking for an explanation, they will interpret it according to their own notions of what is meant. Instances of blunders daily occur from this source. Similar mistakes may also arise from Europeans overrating their own knowledge of the native languages.

Attention and kindness to the natives, and the exercise of justice towards them, will secure their confidence and affection, which must prove of great advantage to the officers acting with them individually, and to the country at large.

Whilst we are lords of the coast, and every person bows to our will, these considerations are of the less importance. But if it should be our fate to contend for our Eastern possessions, against a powerful, active, and intriguing European enemy, it is then we shall derive advantages from the confidence and attachment of the natives.

Appendix

Made June 27, 1803, before Captain Madge and Captain Pierce, of the 19th Regiment, and Assistant-Surgeon Gillespie, of the Malay Regiment

That on the 23rd June, a little before daylight, the Candians commenced an attack on the hill guard, in rear of the palace, on which was a 3-pounder, and took it. That soon after a strong body of the enemy, headed by a Malay chief, made a charge on the eastern barrier, to endeavour to take a gun which was there; they were opposed by Lieutenant Blakeney, at the head of a few men of the 19th, who himself fell in the conflict. That an incessant fire was kept up until two o'clock in the day, when, as the enemy was endeavouring to break in at the rear of the palace, Major Davie hung out a flag of truce, offering to surrender the town, on being permitted to march out with his arms. This they consented to; and Major Davie, after spiking the guns, marched out about five o'clock, and proceeded to Wattapologo, where he was obliged to halt all night, being unable to pass the river. Next morning the Candians sent out four *Modiliars* to propose, that if Major Davie would give up Boodoo Sawmy (the king whom Governor North placed on the throne of Candy, and who retreated with our troops), they would assist him with boats and rafts to cross the river; on which Major Davie gave him up by his own consent. After which another message was sent, that there were plenty of bamboos and other materials at hand, and they might make rafts for themselves. All that day was employed in endeavouring to make rafts, but they could not succeed in getting a rope across the river, owing to the depth and rapidity of the current; but next day, about ten o'clock,

Captain Humphreys, of the Bengal artillery, came and reported that he had succeeded in getting a rope across.

About this time some of the Malays and gun *lascars* began to desert in small parties; upon which Major Davie ordered the remainder to ground their arms and follow him, with all the officers, back to the garrison. As soon as they had proceeded two hundred yards on their way thither, the Candians stopped them, took the officers on one side, and kept them prisoners for half-an-hour; when this declarent says, he heard shot in the direction of the place where the officers were prisoners, and which was followed by their massacre.

That immediately after, they took the European soldiers two by two, and leading them a few yards along the road, knocked them down with the butt end of their pieces, and beat out their brains. That this declarent was also led out with his comrade, and received a blow under the right ear, and a wound on the back of his neck, which the enemy conceiving to be sufficient, then proceeded to the murder of the remainder. That he lay as dead for some time, and in that situation distinctly heard the firing, which he supposes to be the putting them all to death. That he took the opportunity, while this was doing, of crawling into the jungle, (forest), where he lay till night, and then proceeded to Fort Macdowal to give the information to Captain Madge.

(Signed)

George X Barnsley,
Corporal, 19th Regiment.

Extract from History of Ceylon

Contents

Trincomalee Taken by the English

The British appear to have cast their eyes upon Ceylon with a desire of conquering it, for the first time in 1766. Their power had now become formidable in the east, and the advantages which the Dutch derived from the possession of the harbour of Trincomalee could not be hidden from the presidential governments of India. The motive for their interference during that year is obvious and plain; but no sense of interest should have blinded them to the injustice of such a proceeding. The Dutch were then involved in a bloody and destructive war with the native prince, but they were at peace with England, and there was therefore no excuse for the interference of the latter power. Interest and justice, however, are not always combined in the operations of powerful kingdoms, and accordingly, in 1766, Mr Pybus arrived at the court of Candy, on a mission from the British Government of Madras. He was instructed to assure the king of the friendship of the English; to represent, in lively terms, the rapid growth, and wide extent of their Indian territories, and to offer him suitable supplies to conduct the war against the Dutch. The subsequent neglect of this treaty by the Madras government, however, defeated the intentions of the embassy, and left no favourable impression on the Candian mind of our fidelity or justice.

Towards the conclusion of the American war, in 1782, another, and a more formidable attempt was made by the British governor of Madras upon the island. A fleet under the command of Admiral Sir Edward Hughes, and a body of land forces under that of Sir Hector Munro, were accordingly despatched by Lord Macartney to reduce the Ceylonese possessions of the Dutch, a war then raging between us and that power. An ambassador to the Candian court, Mr Hugh Boyd [1], was also despatched with the expedition, to enter into a treaty

---

1. One of the reputed authors of Junius' Letters.

of peace with the king, and to remove, if possible, his unfavourable opinion of the British.

The fort of Trincomalee was quickly taken on the morning subsequent to their arrival, and Mr Boyd was shortly after despatched on his mission. In the meantime, the admiral thought it necessary to sail for Madras, in order to execute some repairs, and on again reaching the noble harbour which he had so lately left, he perceived French colours flying on the fort, and a French fleet in possession of the bay, in which position he was obliged to leave it.

Mr Boyd has left us in his works, (see note following), a particular account of this extraordinary embassy. Such was the inaccessible nature of the country, that, although travelling with all the speed circumstances would allow, he did not reach Candy, distant 172 miles from Trincomalee by the route which he took, till the fourth of March, having left the latter fort on the fifth of February. The country in that direction was, as it still is, in a wretched condition. Occasionally a tolerable pathway was to be met with, but generally they had to force their way through an almost impervious forest, inaccessible even to the light of heaven. Scenes of the richest and most sublime character were not wanting, however, to diversify the journey, but every where a lamentable deficiency of inhabitants exemplified the almost ruined state of the country. Arrived at Candy, he was met with tedious conferences, and vexatious delays, and it was not till the seventeenth of March that he was released from attendance in the Candian court, to fall into the hands of the French on his return.

★★★★★★

Note:—*Miscellaneous Works of Hugh Boyd*, vol. ii. The following is a copy of the letter addressed by Mr Boyd to Rajadhi Rajah Singha, previous to his departure from Trincomalee: To the King of Candy, &c., &c., from Hugh Boyd, Esq., &c.

I have the honour of acquainting your Highness, that I am appointed ambassador to your Highness' *Durbar*, by his Excellency the Right Honourable Lord Macartney, the Governor, and the Presidency of Madras; and that I am charged with a letter to your Highness, from the governor, in order to explain to you their favourable sentiments, and assure you of their friendship. I suppose your Highness has already heard of the great successes of the English against their enemies, particularly the Dutch, whom they have now driven entirely from the coast of Coromandel, having taken from them their last settlement there, Negapatam.

To carry on the victories of the English against the Dutch, Vice-admiral Sir Edward Hughes, commander-in-chief of the King of England's ships and marine forces in India, is now arrived with the fleet and force under his command at Trincomalee, in conjunction with the troops of the English East India Company. He has already taken one of their forts from the Dutch, called Trincomalee fort, with many prisoners, and without opposition. And he is proceeding with equal vigour, and with certainty of equal success against their only other fort, called Ostendburgh, which must also yield to the great superiority of the British arms.

This will certainly have been effected long before your Highness can have received this letter. But in the character with which I have the honour of being invested as ambassador to your Highness, I am desirous to take the earliest opportunity in transmitting to you these happy particulars, to assure you that it is only against their enemies, the Dutch, that the arms of the English are directed; and that the highest respect and attention will be shewn to your Highness' rights and dignity, and that your subjects will be treated with the utmost kindness and friendship, according to a declaration which His Excellency. Sir Edward Hughes, Admiral and Commander-in-Chief, has already published. I am happy in communicating these matters to your Highness, not doubting that it will give you pleasure to hear of the success and power of your friends.

As many more English ships and troops are expected soon to be here, and as some great further operations will probably be soon carried on by them, for the destruction of their enemies, and the advantage of their friends, I am ordered by his Excellency, the Governor of Madras, to communicate to your Highness, as soon as possible, the letter from him which I have the honour of being charged with.

I shall be happy, therefore, to deliver it to your Highness in person, with every explanation and friendly assurance which you can desire, as soon as I shall know in reply to this that you have given the necessary orders for my accommodation on the road to Candy, and that you have sent proper persons to conduct me thither. And this, I hope, your Highness will be pleased to do immediately, as there ought to be no delay in transactions of so much importance.

I am also charged with a letter to your Highness, from his Highness Walah Jah, Nabob of the Carnatic, which I shall be happy to deliver to you.

I only wait to have the honour of hearing from your Highness, as I have desired; I shall then immediately proceed to enter on all these important matters, on the most friendly and satisfactory ground to your Highness.

(Signed)   Hugh Boyd.

★★★★★★

To enter into the *minutiae* of his communication with the Candian court would be tedious and unnecessary. Accustomed to bad faith and perfidy from Europeans, the courtiers of Rajadhi naturally treated his offers and professions with distrust. They said:

"Twenty years ago, you sent an ambassador to us when we were at war with the Dutch; your proffers of assistance were answered with unsuspicious openness, and on the departure of your ambassador we heard no more of you or of your offers. *Now* you are at war with that nation; anxious to injure them you come to offer us your assistance to drive them from our island, and you profess to be about to yield us that assistance from the most disinterested motives."

Boyd appealed to the known integrity of British proceedings, but all his pleading was in vain, and, although he flattered himself that he had removed their prejudices against his nation, he was unable to conclude a treaty or to persuade them into an alliance. Such was the result of this second interference with Ceylon.

The Dutch, as we have previously seen, did not acquire their possessions in the island without the exercise of much bravery and perseverance. At Colombo, at Galle, and at Jaffna, the reception which the Portuguese gave them, with their reduced forces, was honourably and manly. There seems no reason, therefore, for the imputation frequently cast upon them, that they had degenerated from the Portuguese of former days. Such, however, cannot be said of the Dutch. They acquired the island by valour and perseverance; they lost it by want of discipline, by turbulence, and pusillanimity. Nothing could be more favourable for the success of the British arms in 1795 than the disorganised state of the Dutch troops. Divided into parties, disunited and mutinous, they filled the different forts which they possessed with debauchery, conspiracies and rebellion, so that it would have been utterly impossible for the Dutch commanders, had they possessed the courage, to make any effectual resistance.

On the union of Holland with the French republic in 1795, war having been declared with that country, the English prepared for a more effectual and certain means of reducing the island. General Stewart was, in that year, sent by the government of Madras with a pretty considerable force to attempt the reduction of Trincomalee. His operations were conducted with great vigour; and after a regular siege of three weeks, the fortress was delivered up by the Dutch commander, just as the invaders were preparing to storm it. Such was the only attempt at resistance made by the Dutch to the British invaders of Ceylon. After refreshing his wearied troops in Trincomalee, General Stewart next advanced round the north of the island to Jaffna, which was surrendered by its commandant on the first summons.

Early in 1796, the indefatigable general appeared before Negombo, and it, too, like Jaffna, was at once surrendered.

His eyes were next turned upon Colombo, the strength of whose fortress, and the extent of whose garrison, seemed to promise a lengthened siege. With three regiments of the line (52nd, 73rd and 77th), three battalions of *sepoys*, and a detachment of Bengal artillery, Stewart set out for its reduction. Dangerous woods and rapid rivers were to be crossed before they reached their destination, but not an ambuscade obstructed their march, not an attempt was made to interrupt their advance. At the River Kalany, four miles from the fort, where the stream was broad and deep, and defended by a fort erected on its southern bank, the English halted, expecting the commencement of a difficult and bloody struggle. Two days had scarcely elapsed, however, ere they heard, to their astonishment, that the guns were dismounted, the fort evacuated, and that its defenders had retreated to Colombo.

With caution and anxiety the river was crossed, an encampment formed, and the siege planned. The cowardly occupants of Colombo made but one attempt to defend it: *a body of Malays, headed by a Frenchman*, were sent against the invaders, but were obliged to retreat with precipitation after the loss of their commander. In a few days a capitulation was concluded, and the capital of the maritime provinces was surrendered without a struggle,[2] whilst the other forts in the island

---

2. The Dutch force consisted of two battalions of Hollanders, the French regiment of Wirtemberg, with some native troops, forming in all a force equal to that of the invaders.—Percival.

speedily followed the example of the capital.

The total want of discipline amongst the Dutch troops, and their mutinous insubordination, were perhaps die most powerful aids which the British possessed. Even the life of their commander and governor was often endangered by the outrageous conduct of his troops. To this cause, then, and to a total want of energy and courage in their commanders, we must attribute the easy conquest and occupation of Ceylon by the British troops.

Such was the conclusion of the third great act in the drama of Ceylonese history.

The coasts having thus come into the possession of the English, no time was lost in endeavouring to conciliate the native prince, and to establish a peace on a sure and secure foundation. An ambassador was at once despatched to the Candian court, whilst Rajadhi, in his turn, sent one to Madras. The government of Fort St George, through the medium of Mr Andrews, offered to the Candians privileges and advantages which they had not quietly enjoyed for the preceding two hundred years. The leways or salt marshes of Putlam were to be delivered into their hands, and ten vessels were to be allowed his Candian majesty for foreign and domestic commerce, exempt from all European supervision. The treaty, thus apparently concluded, was ratified and signed by the governor of Fort St George, but Rajadhi, with that inexplicable caprice so common in the proceedings of the Ceylonese monarchs, refused to sanction it, (Cordiner's *Ceylon*, vol. ii.).

A slight alteration in the system of jurisdiction on the coast, introduced by the Madras government, had well nigh produced a simultaneous and resolute revolt of the conquered provinces. Malabar *Dubashes*, or agents of the executive, were placed by the collectors of the Civil Service in the situations formerly occupied by the headmen of the Ceylonese, a measure which caused numerous petty insurrections and revolts, which immediately ceased, however, on the restoration of the native officers.

In 1798 the death of Rajadhi Rajah Singha, after a peaceful reign of twenty years, produced an important revolution in the Candian court:

> He bore the character of an indolent, voluptuous man, addicted to love and poetry, and devoted to nothing else.—Davy's *Ceylon*

The following is the description of him given by Mr Hugh Boyd in his account of the embassy in which he was engaged:

He is about thirty-six or thirty-seven years of age, of a grand
majestic appearance; a very large man, and very black, but of
an open intelligent countenance, as I found afterwards on a
nearer approach. On the whole, his figure and attitude put me
much in mind of our Harry the Eighth. He wore a large crown,
which is a very important distinction from the other princes of
the East.—*Miscellaneous Works*, vol. *ii*.

Though he had five queens, he died childless.

The overweening influence of Pilámè Talawé, the first *adigar*, or
prime minister, enabled him to place upon the throne a Malabar youth
of inferior rank [3] to the exclusion of all the royal family. This measure
the second *Adigar* resolutely opposed, and generously sacrificed his life
to what he was convinced was his duty. The principal queen of Rajadhi, with many of his relations, were immediately thrown into prison,
whilst others, including the queen's brother, Mootu Sámy, fled to the
English, and were protected at Jaffna. Sree Wickrama Rajah Singha,
as the young prince was styled on his accession, was, as we may easily
conceive, but a puppet placed upon the throne, the wires of which
were held and directed by the ambitious Talawé.

In 1798, Mr North [4] arrived from Madras to undertake the government of the island, and early in the following year he had an inter-
view with the prime minister. At first Talawé had not the effrontery
to unmask his treasonable and vicious designs, but in a subsequent
conference, he openly offered, if assisted by the English, to take away
the life of his sovereign, and to rule the country in subjection to his
coadjutors. The infamous proposal was treated with merited scorn,
and several subsequent communications to the same effect shared the
same fate.

These representations, however, were not without their effect on
Mr North's mind; although decency forbade his openly harbouring
the design, interest urged him to prosecute a similar one in a more
secret manner, and by apparently an honourable line of conduct. This
fully appears from the instructions with which General Macdowall
was deputed to the Candian court. The Reverend Mr Cordiner says;

In order to elude the arts of the *Adigar*, the governor promised

---

3. He was, however, a kind of half-nephew to Rajadhi, being a son of a sister of a
concubine of that prince.
4. Afterwards the Earl of Guildford.

that Major-General Macdowall should be sent as an ambassador, if the consent of the king were previously obtained to his carrying with him a sufficient military force to maintain his independence. *It was at the same time proposed that, if the king should approve of it, he should transport his person and his court, for greater safety, to the British territories, there to enjoy all his royal rights, and to depute to Pilámè Talawé, the Adigar, the exercise of his power in Candy.*

All this, then, was proposed "to elude the arts of the *Adigar!*"

The embassy was, with the permission of the Candian court, accordingly despatched. More like a military expedition [5] than a friendly deputation, it was frequently obliged to quell the rebellious natives who opposed its progress, and, after an ineffectual and protracted discussion, it returned without having effected the slightest alteration in the connection between the two powers.

In April 1802, a pretext was found for sending troops into the Candian dominions. Some Mahommedan merchants having been plundered of a quantity of *areka* nuts by a party of Candians, a demand was made by the British governor for restitution. This the court of Wickrama Singha, or his director, Pilámè Talawé, promised to give, but after repeated evasions of the demand, Mr North resolved to extort it by force. Major-General Macdowall was therefore put at the head of a considerable force,[6] and left Colombo for Candy on the last day of January 1803. On the 4th of February, Colonel Barbut [7] set out from Trincomalee with the same intention, and both detachments, after an unresisted march, arrived, "almost at the same moment," at the capital of Ceylon. This they found totally deserted; and accordingly, the combined forces, consisting altogether of upwards of 3000 men, took peaceable possession of it.

---

5. The escort consisted of the light company and four battalions of His Majesty's 19th Foot, five companies of the second battalion of the 6th regiment of coast *sepoys*, five companies of the Malay regiment, a detachment from the Bengal artillery, with four six pounders and two howitzers, and part of the Madras pioneer and Lavar corps.—Percival.

6. This force consisted of two incomplete companies of the Bengal artillery, with the usual proportion of gun lascars, two companies of His Majesty's 19th regiment of Foot, the entire 61st regiment, (625 strong,) 1000 Ceylon native infantry, one company of Malays, and a small corps of pioneers.

7. The force under Col. Barbut comprehended "one company of the Madras artillery, fire companies of the 19th foot, the greater part of the Malay regiment, and a necessary proportion of *lascars* and pioneers."—Cordiner, vol. ii. part ii. ch. i.

They found the palace partly destroyed by fire, those apartments which remained being ornamented with "sets of glass and china ware, and a few golden cups adorned with silver filigree." There were also pier-glasses and statues, particularly of Buddha, and the arsenals were well supplied with warlike instruments of the most heterogeneous kind.

The Candian court being resolutely bent on resistance, the next proceeding of Mr North was to send Mootu Sámy (whom we formerly mentioned as having fled to his protection) to Candy, and there to have him formally crowned king. A treaty was then entered into with him, which, as may be readily conceived, was not very disadvantageous to the British interests. This treaty stipulated that full indemnity should be done the British for all the losses hitherto sustained by its merchants and soldiers; that a tract of land, stretching directly through the centre of his Candian Majesty's dominions, should be yielded to the invaders, for the purpose of constructing a road between Colombo and Trincomalee, doubtless with a disinterested desire for the improvement of the country; that the district of the Seven Korles, a tract along the western coast, should be given up in perpetuity to the English, His Candian Majesty's dominions being already more extensive than he could well govern; and that the king should enter into treaty with no foreign power without His Britannic Majesty's consent; whilst the British, on their part, generously promised, in return for these concessions, to keep a European force continually in Candy, for the greater security of His Candian Majesty's person.

In this manner, arrangements were made *with the most sincere cordiality* between the British Government and Mootu Sámy.—Cordiner.

The operations of Pilámè in opposition to the English were cunning and efficacious. Aware of the great inferiority of his troops in a regular engagement, he kept hovering about Candy, with the design of starving the invaders, or of reducing them to distress by stratagem. By artful representations he succeeded in getting a detachment sent under the command of Col. Barbut to Hangramketty, a fortress situated sixteen miles south-east of Candy, in a hilly and inaccessible district; and were it not for the timely apprehensions of the commander, probably not a man would have returned to recount the disaster. Candy was now a blockaded town. All communication with Colombo and Trincomalee was cut off; the mail from the former town was inter-

cepted, and a detachment sent out to conciliate the neighbouring no-
blemen was narrowly saved from destruction by a precipitate retreat.
Ten *rupees* were offered by the politic Talawé for the head of every
European which might be brought him, and half that sum for that of
any of the auxiliaries. In this state matters continued for some time,
(the English occasionally breaking through the lines of the Ceylonese,
and conveying food to the garrison of Candy,) without either party
gaining any signal advantage. About the commencement of the rainy
season in March and April, negotiations were again opened between
the belligerent parties, Talawé's intention apparently being to keep the
troops as long as possible in Candy, well aware that sickness would,
sooner or later, thin their ranks. In these renewed conferences, the
Adigar promised to deliver up the so-called king to the British, and
to allow a suitable maintenance to Mootu Sámy at Jaffna, on condition that the chief power and viceroyalty of Candy might be vested in
himself, under the title of *Ootoon Komarayan*, or Great Prince.

The infamous proposal was agreed to by General Macdowall, the
British commander, who, relying upon the honour of the faithless and
perjured Pilámè, left Candy for Colombo with a considerable detachment of the troops, another party directing their march to Trincomalee, leaving the garrison of Candy under Major Davie, about 1000
strong. Such a measure was evidently exceedingly reprehensible: why
should so small a force have been left in the midst of a hostile country
under such a commander? and how could the British expect, that he
who was neither faithful to his country nor his king, would be faithful
to his enemies?

The next attempt of the first *Adigar* was, to get possession of the
person of Mr North. For this purpose, a conference was proposed at
Dambadiva, formerly the royal residence, fifty-six miles east of Colombo, to which Mr North, anxious to promote peace, at once ac-
ceded. He went, however, attended by a strong guard, whilst another
of 300 men unexpectedly met him from Candy. This circumstance
probably saved him from confinement; Talawé was afraid to put his
treacherous project into execution in the face of such an escort, and,
after a fruitless ratification of the former treaty, the two commanders
separated.

The troops in Candy were suffering daily from fever and desertion.
Large parties of the Candian forces were continually hovering in their
vicinity; and towards the latter end of June, a formidable attack was
made upon the enfeebled garrison. Major Davie, unable effectually to

resist, proposed an armistice, and a truce was agreed to, on condition that he should at once deliver up Candy, with all its military stores, to the *Adigar*, whilst the British troops, retaining their arms, should march to Trincomalee. During this and the previous transactions, we cannot ascribe too much praise to the noble conduct of Captain Nouradeen, the native commander of the Malay forces. Tempted with the most flattering offers by the native princes in the opposite army, he still maintained his integrity, and has left a noble instance of the faithfulness and fidelity of his nation.

On the evening of the day on which the surrender had been made, Major Davie and Captain Nouradeen marched from Candy at the head of upwards of four hundred men, fourteen of whom were British officers, leaving 120 sick Europeans to the tender mercies of their savage enemies. Scarcely had they advanced two miles, when the Mahavelli-ganga, a rapid and considerable stream, then swollen with the rain, opposed their progress. There were no means of crossing it: it had been completely forgotten in the capitulation, and the destitute followers of Major Davie stood in irresolution, whilst their taunting enemies occupied the neighbouring hills. Their attempts to provide rafts on the following morning were totally unsuccessful; and at length some Candian chiefs entered into communication with Major Davie and his baffled fellow-officers.

The degrading proposal was made to them of delivering up the unfortunate Mootu Sámy to his enemies, on which condition alone boats would be provided. After some delay and hesitation this base, this infamous proceeding was agreed to, and Major Davie himself communicated the tidings to the unhappy prince. "My God," was his exclamation, "is it possible that the triumphant arms of England can be so humbled, as to fear the menaces of such cowards as the Candians." His expostulations were lost upon the pusillanimous officer whom he addressed, and Mootu Sámy was accordingly delivered to his enemies, a human sacrifice offered up by British soldiers to the demon of Candian cruelty.

Led before Wickrama Singha, he was asked, "was it proper for you, being, as you are, of the royal family to join the English?"

"I am at the king's mercy," was his humble reply.

A few more questions were asked and answered, after which this unfortunate victim of British cowardice suffered the most dreadful and barbarous of all deaths—impalement.

It would have been strange, indeed, if this act of Major Davie's had benefited his troops. That cowardice and cruelty usually go hand-in-hand was fully proved in the present instance. Conscious of their power from the two previous submissions, the next demand of the Candians was that the British troops and their allies should return unarmed to Candy. Every thing was agreed to,—Major Davie and his officers were separated from the troops,—the latter were marched into a narrow defile, — they were then taken out two by two, and, in cold blood, massacred by the Caffres in the Candian service, each successive pair being led to a distance from the larger company, and then murdered. The entire body of helpless sick left in the hospital soon after shared the same fate. But three European officers were spared alive (Major Dayie, Captain Burnley and Captain Humphreys), and these ended their lives afterwards in miserable captivity.

Such were the fearful effects of the misconduct of Major Davie, misconduct fortunately rare in the annals of British warfare, and which was awfully visited on his own and his brother-officers' heads. To attempt any palliation of his conduct would be futile and useless. That death is ever, and under all circumstances, preferable to infidelity and dishonour, is a maxim of which every soldier should be convinced, and without which no man has a right to take upon him a military command. What might not resolution and decision have accomplished under the circumstances in which he was placed? [8] And if victory or death had been steadily placed before his mind would he not have gained immortal honour in either case? In the former, respect and admiration during life, and an honourable name in the pages of history after it; in the latter, a no less honourable death, and the same reward subsequently.

The darkest shades, however, are seldom without some bright spot to relieve them; and it is grateful to turn from the pusillanimity of one officer, (although a Briton), to the devotion and heroism of another, and a Malay. We have already noticed the decision and fidelity of Captain Nouradeen, in his former transactions with the Candians, as an enemy; and as a captive, we shall find the same consistency persevered in with admirable strength of mind. Life, service, honours and command were offered to him if he would desert the English standard and join that of Wickrama Singha, but he resolutely refused, declaring that he was already the servant of a great king, and that he could not serve

---

8. That this is not merely an unmeaning rhetorical flourish, the example of Major Johnson in 1804, on a similar emergency, to be afterwards alluded to, incontestably proves.

two masters. He was accordingly beheaded.

Elated by these successes, the king now meditated the entire expulsion of the English, and prepared forces for a general and simultaneous attack upon the various provinces under their dominion. Even
Colombo itself was threatened, but his Candian Majesty found that
even the inconsiderable fort of Hangwelle, when resolutely defended,
was more than sufficient to embarrass all his designs. Amidst the mass
of petty actions continued during the years of 1804 and 1805, which
it would be equally tedious and uninteresting to particularise,[9] the
expedition of Major[10] Johnson into the interior alone deserves our
attention. With a body of 300 troops, attended by a large train of
coolies and servants, he fought his way from Batticaloa to Candy, was
there surrounded by the Candian forces, and thence marched with
continual skirmishing to Trincomalee, thus triumphantly exhibiting
what valour and perseverance could accomplish when headed by tal-
ent and decision.

The war which continued during these years was carried on with
great cruelty on both sides. It was, in fact, a system of retaliation and
reprisal which no country could long endure. Accordingly, in 1805,
the king, doubtless finding himself unable to prosecute it, made over-
tures for an armistice, which, without any formal treaty, was continued
from that year till 1814.[11] The ten years which intervened, however,
were by no means without producing important events in the government of Candy.

The terms on which Pilámè Talawé and Wickrama Singha had so
long acted together, during a protracted war, could not be continued
on the same footing, during the lengthened peace which succeeded
it. The authority which the minister had possessed during the previous part of the reign he could not reasonably expect to enjoy during a
time of profound peace. Scarcely had a year elapsed ere circumstances
intervened to disturb their co-operation; and although they did not
then come to an open rupture, the seeds of dissension and animosity
were sown, and required but time to bring forth their pernicious fruit.
The king was determined on governing with absolute power, and

9. The curious reader will find every incident of this war related in Cordiner's *Ceylon*, vol. ii. part ii. chap. 4.
10. Subsequently Lieutenant-Colonel. He published a narrative of this expedition.
London, 1810.
11. In 1805, the Honourable F. North, to whose abilities the English are indebted
for Ceylon, was succeeded by Sir Thomas Maitland in the government of the island,
who, in 1812, was, in his turn, succeeded by Sir Robert Brownrigg.

Pilámè, on his part, was *as* determined to maintain his influence.

A censure passed on the works in which the sovereign was engaged called forth from him some angry words, which raised the fears and excited the hatred of the minister. A few years passed in this state of mutual jealousy, when a request of Pilámè to be allowed to marry his son to the illegitimate daughter of the last king excited the apprehensions of the king. Unable to repress his indignation at what he conceived to be an open attempt at the sovereignty, the king assembled the chiefs, brought several charges against the minister, and having fully condemned him, expressed his unwillingness to injure one to whom he was so much attached, and accordingly forgave him. Whether this latter measure was dictated by a spirit of crafty subtlety, or whether it was the generous emotion of a mind not wholly abandoned, cannot now be determined. Certain it is, that the enmity of the king was soon rekindled, and Pilámè , deprived of all his honours and offices, was sent to live as a private individual in his own province.

The resentment of Pilámè, for this treatment, was not long in exhibiting itself. Malay assassins were hired to despatch the king, a rebellion was fomented, and, on the failure of both enterprises, the ex-minister and his nephew [12] were beheaded, (*a. d.* 1812.) Pilámè was succeeded in the office of prime minister by Eheylapola, formerly the second *Adigar*. No conduct on the part of the minister, however faithful and devoted, could allay the suspicions of the monarch. Eheylapola had scarcely been raised to the vacant dignity ere the fears of Wickrama exhibited themselves. Those districts which he considered tainted with the leaven of rebellion were treated with a harshness and severity sufficient to excite it, in subjects the most loyal. All priests, and the Moors or merchants, were ordered to leave them by a stated time, whilst, with a needless rigour, no women who were not natives of the provinces were allowed to remain in them. The effect of this order may easily be conceived:

> . . . . wives were separated from their husbands, mothers from their children; the young bride and the aged parent, all, indiscriminately, were torn from the bosom of their families, and driven from their homes; producing scenes of distress and feelings of anger, which might well shake the firmest loyalty.—Dr. Davy's *Ceylon*.

---

12. His son, who was spared from an accidental delay, we shall afterwards find actively engaged against the English.

The enmity of the king towards his prime minister was not long in displaying itself. The trifling occasion of the presentation of a gift was sufficient to make him display his resentment and jealousy, and on the return of Eheylapola to his own district, Saffragam, (in the Southern Province, where he was almost adored,) his conduct left no doubt on the mind of the king of his rebellious intentions. Saffragam was soon in a state of open rebellion, a correspondence was carried on with Colombo, and active measures taken to procure the dethronement of the tyrant. Wickrama Singha was not idle on hearing of these proceedings. The second Adigar, Molligodde, was at once despatched against Eheylapola with a competent force, and, before his departure, he was formally installed in all the honours of the rebel. Eheylapola was obliged to betake himself to Colombo, his adherents were dispersed, and Molligodde returned in triumph to Candy.

Nothing could exceed the fury of the king on this second rebellion of his chief officer, and his anger was fearfully visited on the heads of all those suspected of the slightest misdemeanours. Impalements, tortures, and beheading, succeeded each other in quick rotation, and scarcely had one been executed ere another was doomed to succeed him. The final scene of this domestic barbarity was horrible in the extreme, and if we wound the feelings of our readers by relating it, we must be excused by our strict adherence to truth, προς ταυτα κρυπτε μηδεν.

The unfortunate wife and children of Eheylapola were still in Candy, and under the power of the inhuman tyrant whose actions we are relating. They were condemned to die. Before one of the temples of the gods, in the market-place of Candy, they were doomed to suffer, and were led forth by the gaoler who had them in charge. The lady advanced to meet her fate with resolution; she proclaimed the legality of her lord's conduct, and her own innocence, and hoped that the present sacrifice might be for his good. She then told her eldest boy, a lad of eleven years old, to submit to his fate; the poor infant recoiled with horror from the sacrifice, when his noble brother, two years younger, stepped forwards with a determined mien, and told him that *he* would shew him how to die. One blow was struck and the head of the youthful hero was rolling at their feet.

The barbarity was not to end here however. The severed head was thrown into a rice mortar, the pestle was placed in the hand of the unfortunate mother, and she was told that if she refused to use it *she should be disgracefully tortured*. The poor woman stood for a moment in irresolution, but disgrace was worse than any inward struggle. She lifted the pestle up, and once she let it fall. The unfortunate woman's sufferings did not end here. One by one the same harrowing scene was repeated, until all were gone, and at last the poor infant at her breast was torn from its resting place, where, in unconscious innocence, it knew nothing of the awful scene that was transacting around it. It too was beheaded, and the milk which it had just received flowed forth to mingle with its blood. For the honour of human nature we must add, that:

.....during this tragical scene, the crowd who had assembled to witness it wept and sobbed aloud, unable to suppress their feelings. Palihapanè Dissava was so affected that he fainted, and was expelled his office for shewing such tender sensibility. During two days the whole of Candy, with the exception of the tyrant's court, was as one house of mourning and lamentation; and so deep was the grief, that not a fire (it is said) was kindled, no food was dressed, and a general fast was held.

To relate particular instances of the further cruelty of the king would be useless, if not disgusting. The above is but a fair specimen of this Candian reign of terror.

The English were not uninterested regarders of these events. Towards the conclusion of 1814, the year in which the barbarity just related was executed on the wife of Eheylapola, the British forces were prepared for an invasion of the Candian territories, and a cause for declaring war was not long wanting. Some merchants from the British territories trading to the interior were shamefully treated by the Candian tyrant, and came in a mutilated condition to complain to the government at Colombo. Accordingly, on the 10th January 1815, (a year memorable in Ceylonese as in European history,) a proclamation of war was sent forth, not against the Candian territory or nation, but:

. . .against that tyrannical power which had provoked, by aggravated outrages and indignities, the just resentment of the British nation, which had cut off the most ancient and noble families in the kingdom, deluged the land with the blood of its subjects, and, by the violation of every religious and moral law, had become an object of abhorrence to mankind.

The troops were at once marched from all quarters upon the territory of the tyrant; a series of desultory and uninteresting combats ensued; the Candians fought, not as men defending their country and their liberty from hostile invasion, but as men compelled by the sovereign fiat of a cruel tyrant to take arms against their friends. The result of such a contest could not be doubtful; but it was rendered indisputably in the favour of the English, by the desertion, from the king, of the only able general whom he possessed. As long as his wife and family remained in Candy, Molligodde, warned by the fate of Eheylapola, could not desert, but no sooner had they made their escape than he hastened to present himself to the British, as a hater of the tyrant, and a friend of any who would dethrone him.[13] This event happened on the 8th of February, and on the 14th of the same month the headquarters of General Brownrigg were established in Candy. The king had, unfortunately, fled thence a few days previous, and it was generally believed that his flight had been directed towards the Dombera province, ten or twelve miles distant.

This supposition amounted to certainty, on Major Kelly's division, which was advancing to the capital from that quarter, having fallen in with two of the king's wives and a large treasure, on the same day that Candy had been entered. Plans were now proposed and adopted for the capture of Wickrama, the great end of all the previous measures. Detachments from Major Hook's and Colonel O' Council's divisions were sent to scour the country around; but had not the natives interested themselves in the capture, probably all the exertions of the English had been vain. A party of Eheylapola's followers, assisted by some of the inhabitants of the district, at length succeeded in discovering and securing the refugee prince. He was well defended by the Malabar escort which he carried with him, but they being finally overpowered, he was captured on the 18th February 1815, the day from which we may date the extinction of Ceylonese independence, an independence which had continued, without any material interruption, for 2357 years.[14]—Sic transit gloria mundi.

---

13. Vide a Journal and Narrative of the Military Operations in Ceylon in 1815, by an officer employed in the expedition." Ceylon Miscellany, vol. i.
14. The king was conveyed early in the following year to Madras, whence be was subsequently removed to Vellore, where he died on the 30th January 1832, of dropsy.

Conclusion

The treatment which the Candian monarch received from the party who captured him was disgraceful in the extreme. They bound him hand and foot, reviled him as a monster and a tyrant unworthy to draw another breath; dragged him to a neighbouring village with every mark of disgrace; and, to crown the ignominy which he endured, spat upon him as he went. On being delivered to the English, however, he was treated with suitable respect, and he felt grateful for it. Two different accounts have been handed down to us of his appearance and character, neither of which appears in unison with what his actions would lead us to expect. An officer engaged in the embassy to Candy in 1800 has left us the following portrait of him:

> The king seemed very vain of his dress, and very uneasy on his throne; he kept constantly shaking his head to display the precious stones in his crown, and pulled down his vest or armour to shew off the jewels with which it was studded. He seemed particularly fond of a large round ornament which is suspended from his neck.—*Cordiner* vol. ii.

From this portrait of an idiot, we turn with surprise to the following:

> Wickrama Rajah Singha is, in his person, considerably above the middle size; of a corpulent, yet muscular appearance, and with a physiognomy which is at all times handsome, and frequently not unpleasing. His claim to talent has been disputed by many who have had an opportunity of conversing with him, but he is certainly not deficient in shrewdness or comprehension.—A *Narrative of Events, &c.*, by a gentleman engaged in the expedition. Egerton, 1820.

He had certainly disappointed the expectations of his first prime minister, Pilàmè Talawé, a man who had raised him to the throne in the hope of governing him as he pleased, but who found himself fatally mistaken. That he was a cruel savage, a heartless tyrant, and a haughty despot, is plainly proved by his history; and we can now only regret that he should have been so long allowed to rule a generous and ancient people.

A fortnight subsequent to the capture of the king, he was formally dethroned by a convention held on the 2nd March 1816, between His Excellency, the Governor and Commander-in-chief of the forces, and the Chief Officers of the Candian empire. The official bulletin published on the occasion says:

"This day a solemn conference was held in the audience hall of the palace of Candy, between his Excellency, the Governor and Commander-in-chief of the forces, on behalf of his Majesty and of his Royal Highness the Prince Regent, on the one part, and the *Adigars, Dissaves* and other principal chiefs of the Candian provinces, on the other part, on behalf of the people, and in presence of the Mohottales, Coraals, Vidaans and other subordinate headmen from the different provinces, and a great concourse of inhabitants.

A public instrument of treaty, prepared in conformity to conditions previously agreed on, for establishing His Majesty's Government in the Candian provinces, was produced, and publicly read in English and Singhalese, and unanimously assented to. The British flag was then for the first time hoisted, and the establishment of the British dominion in the interior was announced by a royal salute from the cannon of the city.

By the second article of the treaty then entered into, Sri Wickrama Rajah Singha was formally declared to be deposed; his family and relations for ever debarred from the throne, and all the claims of his race to be "extinguished and abolished."

By the fifth, the religion of Buddha was declared "inviolable, and its rights, ministers and places of worship, were to be maintained and protected." By the eighth, the laws of the country were to be still recognised and acted on, "according to established forms, and by the ordinary authorities." And, lastly, by the eleventh, the royal dues and revenues were to be levied as before, for the support of government.

Such were the principal heads of the treaty entered into on the submission of the entire island to the arms of England.

For two years every thing progressed favourably, the natives appeared contented with the government of their new commanders, whilst, on the part of the English, the terms of the agreement were strictly adhered to. A breathing time was thus allowed to the exhausted country, which proved, however, but the lull before the tempest, or the important calm that precedes the sudden attack. One final struggle was still to be made for that independence which Malabars, Malays, Moors, Portuguese and Dutch had all failed to extinguish. The desire was natural, although ungrateful; for as they had assisted the invaders to depose their king, so neither had they expressed the slightest resentment at the treaty that had been concluded. The chiefs, we may easily conceive, would be the first to excite such a revolt. They had no sympathy with their subduers; they had lost their influence; they were now but on a level with their countrymen, and they could become but little less, whatever might chance to be the result of the war.

In October 1817, a spirit of insubordination first exhibited itself in Uva, a hilly district in the south-eastern part of the island. The agent of government stationed there rode forth to repress it, but fell in the attempt, and his escort escaped with difficulty to Badulla, (pronounced Badjula). A priest of Buddha had already thrown off his yellow robes and aspired to the sovereignty, nor was he long without numerous supporters.

The most enterprising chief by whom he was joined, Kapittipola, was the brother-in-law of Eheylapola, and a man of considerable influence in the country. His example, and that of some other influential and powerful leaders, quickly spread the flame just excited, and before six months had elapsed, only a few inconsiderable districts still maintained their allegiance.

During the three following months our affairs assumed a still more melancholy aspect. Our little army was much exhausted and reduced by fatigue, privation and disease; the rebellion was still unchecked; all our efforts had been apparently fruitless; not a leader of any consequence had been taken, and not a district subdued or tranquillised. This was a melancholy time to those who were on the scene of action; and many began to despond and augur from bad to worse; and to prophesy (what indeed was far from improbable) that the few districts still attached to us would join the enemy; that the communication between Colombo and our head quarters at Candy would be cut off, and that we should be very soon obliged to evacuate the country, and fight our way out of it.—Davy's *Ceylon*.

All things end in their contraries, said Socrates, and the present narration does not disprove his assertion. That "*union is strength*" seems to have been forgotten by the Ceylonese chiefs. Dissensions arose amongst them of a serious nature. Their general, Kapittipola, was defeated in several engagements; and to crown their discomfiture the pretender was seized by an opposing party, who immediately erected another as their chief. Under such a state of things it was impossible that their measures could succeed; and whatever successes they met with at first, were more than counterbalanced by their subsequent misfortunes. No conduct on the part of the Ceylonese, however, could justify the cruelty of the English. A district was declared rebellious.

Detachments were sent to scour the country,' to butcher all whom they found with arms in their hands, to destroy and lay waste every thing that came in their way. Dwellings were burned; fruit-tree plantations were cut down, and martial law proclaimed throughout the district. Such proceedings as those may have been politic and successful, but they are not those on which a humane mind can dwell with pleasure, and we may reasonably question, whether it would not have been more just and wise altogether to evacuate the interior than to allow such a state of things to continue for nearly two years.[1]

The loss of the British troops was very severe, nearly a fifth part of their forces having perished by disease alone. The Candians resorted to every species of attack which they could devise, and left no effort untried to bring about the destruction of their foes. Pits were dug with concealed spikes in their road; snares of all kinds, and ambuscades in every practicable place were planted to harass their enemies, and neither mercy nor quarter was given on either side. It was in fact nothing more or less than a war of extermination.

Fortune at length openly declared for skill and discipline. The leaders of the insurrection were captured one by one; and, deprived of their commanders, it was utterly impossible that the natives could support the contest. An event of still greater consequence than even the apprehension of the rebellious princes occurred shortly afterwards,—the capture of the sacred tooth (or Dalada relic) of Buddha. "*Whoever obtain that relic*," says an old Ceylonese tradition, "*obtain with it the Gov-*

---

1. Dr Davy asserts that these "evils" or "irregularities" were not by any means sanctioned by government; but if not directly sanctioned they certainly most have been winked at, or they had never occurred.

ernment of Ceylon;" and, on the information being diffused throughout the country, resistance was at an end, the natives returned to their allegiance, and British rule was once more recognised throughout the entire island. A new convention was at once entered into between the Candian chiefs and Sir R. Brownrigg, stipulating—

> *1st,* That all personal services, excepting those required for making and repairing roads and bridges, should be abolished, and that all taxes should be merged into one,—a tax of one-tenth of the produce of the paddy lands;
>
> *2nd,* That justice should be administered by the Board of Commissioners in Candy, and by the agents of Government in the different provinces, aided by the native *Dissaves,* who were henceforth to be remunerated, not by the contributions of the people, but by fixed salaries. Such was the gratifying conclusion of a struggle which at first threatened the most disastrous consequences; and that the peace which was then concluded may be perpetual is, we trust, the confident hope of every resident in Ceylon.